BE YOUR OWN
MNEY MAKER

Dedicated to...

This book is dedicated to
the Almighty
who is giving me dreams
and showing
me path
to achieve it.

BE YOUR OWN MONEY MAKER

Authored by

MANOJ KR. SINGH

Penman Books

Office No. 303, Kumar House Building,
D Block, Central Market, Opp PVR Cinema,
Prashant Vihar, Delhi 110085, India
Website: www.penmanbooks.com
Email: publish@penmanbooks.com

First Published by Penman Books 2019
Copyright © Manoj Kr. Singh 2019
All Rights Reserved.

Title: Be Your Own Money Maker
Price: ₹399 | $7.99
ISBN: 978-81-940688-0-8

About the Author

anoj Kumar Singh is an Engineer by qualification. He has completed his BE (Electrical) from the prestigious MNNIT, Allahabad, and PGDBM from Bhartiya Vidya Bhawan's Vadodara. He was the recipient of Kulpati award in the Post Graduation.

Manoj is a Certified Project Management Professional of around 25 years of Experience. He has worked with many MNCs as Project Manager. He is a born leader and guided his team to achieve success. He is known for making systemised Learning system for teams. He is a great coach, Mentor and trainer.

His family includes father Shri B.B.Singh, mother Mrs Meena Singh, wife Mamta, daughters Megha, Sonali and son Ishan. He likes to spend time with his family and believes that Positive attitude to learn, Dreams and confidence are the keys to achieve success in any field.

Apart from service, he has good experience of Entrepreneurship and trading. Like any job goer, he started his journey in trading in early 2002 as a hobby and quit trading after losing his capital. He came to know about Technical analysis of Stock trading in 2016 only and found that stock trading is a game of probability and hard work. His journey to become a consistent winner is very inspiring. He found that for becoming consistent winner, you have to acquire deep knowledge of every aspect of trading.

Whenever a person initiates his journey in trading, he becomes very confused as there are many streams, methods, strategies available. This book is written with a view to develop a systematic approach to learn the game of trading. As author himself has gone through each of the learning phases, he simply takes the reader with him and provide methods and ways to remember and apply it easily.

He has trained a lot of beginners to initiate their trading journey in systematic manners. Instead of giving some sure shot formula to gain, his focus is to make you think logically and adopt trading systematically.

~~~
~~~

Preface

First of all, let me congratulate you for your first step to learn Trading. I also welcome you to the journey which we will take together. This book is designed in such a way that it begins at a layman level and goes up to expert level. I am sure that it will help you find the missing link of your success and will show you the way to set it right.

In this book, I have tried to make you think logically so that you can devise your own strategies and apply it. Methods provided in this book are well proven and practiced by successful traders.

I request you to regard this book as working handbook, whenever you find yourself in a long run of losing trades, please go back to the relevant chapters to check where you are going wrong and rectify the mistakes.

This book should not be read in one go. My suggestion is to read the chapter at bird eye level first and then read it again, this time slowly to gain the in depth understanding. Here, I will suggest the beginners to refrain from trading until you complete the book as many topics are interconnected.

In this book we refer to stock trading only but principles can be applied to any security such as currency, commodity etc.

Read this book with a highlighter, crayon, pencil or pen. Keep on marking the points which you like, so that it will be easier for you to come back and refer it again.

The pronoun "he" is used throughout the book. Please take it as he or she as per your gender. Using a single pronoun such as "he" is better and more streamlined to read compared to using slashes in between pronouns like he/she or him/her.

~~~
~~~

Introduction

You can kick your irritating boss and leave your Job, You can survive and work anywhere in the world, You can be independent from the routine and not answerable to anybody...Yes, it can be true... Traders can have the best lifestyle in the world, Can travel to the best locations, can stay in best Hotels, can drink the best brands. Yes, we are discussing about trading in stocks.

But, to succeed in trading you need several innate traits without which you shouldn't even start. They include discipline, risk tolerance, and a keen learning attitude.

Traders make money by buying at Low Price and selling at high Price. If you believe that Market will be going up, you first buy at low price and then sell on high price and If you believe that Market will be going down, you sell first at high Price and buy at low price. (Selling first and buying after, needs margin and can be done intraday only for stocks, However, you can do it in future).

The concept is simple, but implementing it, is difficult.

It is hard to be successful in any profession, but harder to become a good trader. Beginners often assume they can make money because they're smart, can manage teams and have a record of success in their respective Professions. You can get a fast computer and even buy a back tested system from someone, but putting money on it, is like trying to drive a three-wheel rickshaw with two wheels missing. The two other factors are Trader's Psychology and Money Management.

Balancing your mind is just as important as analyzing markets. Your personality influences your perceptions, making it a key aspect of your success or failure. Managing money in your trading account is essential for surviving the inevitable drawdowns and prospering in the long run. Psychology, market analysis, and money management— you have to master all three to become a successful trader.

How long will it take you to become a profitable trader, What rules you need to set, which methods will you use, and how much Capital will you need? What should you study first, second, and third? How much risk to take in each trade and how much money can you expect to make? If you were searching the answers of these questions, you picked the right book. You can succeed in trading. It has been done before by people who started from scratch, learned to trade and are making a good living at it. The best ones make fortunes. Others fail, out of ignorance or lack of discipline. If you work through this book, ignorance will not be a problem. Trading is a journey of self-discovery. If you enjoy learning, if you are not scared of risk, If you are ready to put those extra hours to learn. A rewarding career is awaiting you at the end of the Tunnel.

Let's begin our Journey...

~~~
~~~

Contents

SECTION C: MONEY MANAGEMENT

SECTION D: TRADER'S PSYCHOLOGY

SECTION A

Let's Understand where Trader Fails

CHAPTER 1
Various Trading Failure Scenarios

If you are not an experienced trader, You may find yourself in one of the following scenarios.

SCENARIO 1

You got interested to trade when you saw that one of your friends has just earned a good amount after getting a tip from his stockbroker friend. Next time you had told your friend to inform you whenever he gets the tip. This time you also invested a little from your saving and it resulted in good profit (percentage-wise). Now your confidence is up. You are feeling that now you can fulfil your dreams. You are ready to invest your entire saving. But this time opposite happened and you lost your complete saving. You are not able to understand what went wrong this time.

SCENARIO 2

You are a successful person in your profession and now got interested into investing. You have started listening to CNBC and subscribed to ET. You have just finished reading 3-4 books on trading. You are doing paper trading for last 1 month and now you are confident enough to take on the market. Beginner luck is with you and you just closed your first trade in profit. Based on the percentage return of these two days, you are confident to double your capital in One year. Now your aim is to trade with large Capital. As you are sure that you will double your capital in one year, you have taken a personal loan at 14% interest. You are sure to pay it back in next 1 month. You zeroed on One stock as nearly all of the Experts on CNBC are bullish on it. You invested your entire capital in this stock.

After Day 1, your investment was minor positive and you are feeling happy to take this decision. On Day 2 the stock got into a small negative. But you are not surprised, as many times, the stock goes down first, before rocketing. But Day 3 was a black day and your stock lost 10%. You are now worried and checked CNBC again. Still, experts are bullish on this stock. You decided to hold this stock and within a weeks time, you have lost more than 40% of your capital.

You checked TV channel again and found that Experts on TV channel are declaring this stock a good bargain buy. Now, you are searching for positive news on this stock and also finding the same. But after losing more than 60% of your capital, you are feeling trapped and thinking to come out of it. The very next day Stock dived 10% again and you come out after losing 80% of your capital. Now, you are paying back the loan from your salary.

Enough is enough. You decided that you will never ever invest in the Stock Market.

SCENARIO 3

You are in trading since last one year and recently you observed that there is a lot of over-night risk in trading, hence you are doing intraday trading.

Apart from it, your broker is giving 10 times more exposure on the same margin if you trade intraday. You calculated that even if the stock moves only 2 points, you will be able to take home 20 points profit. After a few initial success, you are now leveraging your Capital 10 times. Suddenly, due to some bad news, your stock falls 8% and you got a margin call from your broker.

As you have already overinvested, your broker squared off your position wiping 90% of your capital in 5 minutes and irony is, that stock again reached its initial value after 1 hour, but now you are left with only 10% of the Capital.

~~~
~~~

CHAPTER 2
How a Novice do the Trading

Often Technical Analysis (TA) is approached as a quick and easy way to make a windfall gain in the markets. On the contrary, technical analysis is anything but quick and easy. Yes, if applied correctly, a large gain is possible but in order to get that stage you need to put in the required effort to learn the technique.

If you approach TA as a quick and easy way to make money in markets, you are bound to lose. When a trading fiasco happens, more often the blame is on technical analysis and not on the trader's inability to efficiently apply Technical Analysis to markets.

Please note that part knowledge is dangerous thing and I will not suggest you to trade unless you complete reading this book. Let us understand it from following example.

Look at the following chart. A novice trader notices the chart of XYZ company at Point 2. He waits to confirm his bullish view and ultimately buy the stock around point 3. He is happy that stock is further moving up. After second day Stock starts falling, but he thinks that such up & down is normal and waits further till point 5, but his view is now becoming bearish. He further waits to confirm and at last, he decides to quit at point 6.

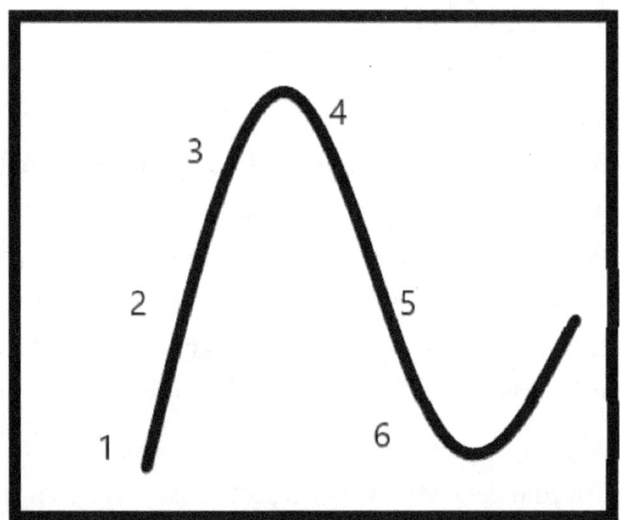

Now understand how smart money works. Smart money buys the stock at point 1 (or point 6) and sells it at point 3. Now think when smart money is selling at point 3, who is buying? it is the retail trader... and the worst part is that so-called Experts on TV are recommending it to buy at this point… Just ask yourself who has the power to influence these experts? A retail trader or Smart money.

Same way when Smart money is buying at point 1 or 6, who is selling them? Now you are correct, it is the retail trader.

~~~
~~~

CHAPTER 3
Common Mistakes in Trading

Before we begin our learning in detail, let us go through the common mistakes made by traders. Though, these mistakes are made by Novice generally, but there is no reason to take it as a rule as I have seen experienced traders also committing the same mistakes. Purpose here is to know beforehand so that you do not fall in the same pit.

Making mistakes is part of the learning process when it comes to trading. Traders generally buy and sell securities more frequently and hold positions for much shorter periods than traditional investors. Such frequent trading and shorter holding periods can result in mistakes that can wipe out a new trader's investing capital quickly.

While traders of all stripes are guilty of the following mistakes from time to time, beginner traders should be especially wary of making them, as their capacity and capability to bounce back from a severe trading setback is likely to be much more restricted than with experienced traders.

LETTING LOSSES MOUNT

One of the defining characteristics of successful traders is their ability to take a small loss quickly if a trade is not working out and move on to the next trade idea. Unsuccessful traders, on the other hand, get paralyzed if a trade goes against them. Rather than taking quick action to cap a loss, they may hold on to a losing position in the hope that the trade will eventually work out. In addition to tying up trading capital for an inordinate period of time in a losing trade, such inaction may result in mounting losses and severe depletion of capital.

AVERAGING DOWN (OR UP) TO REDEEM A LOSING POSITION

Averaging down on a long position in a blue-chip may work for an investor who has a long investment time horizon, but it is not going to work consistently with volatile and riskier securities. Some of the biggest trading losses in history have occurred because a trader kept adding to a losing position, and was eventually forced to cut the entire position when the magnitude of the loss became so huge to carry it further. Traders also go short more often than conservative investors and tend toward "averaging up," because the security is advancing rather than declining. This is an equally risky move that is another common mistake made by the novice trader.

USING TOO MUCH MARGIN OR LEVERAGE

Margin is the use of borrowed money to purchase securities. While margin can help you make more money, it can also exaggerate your losses, making it a definite downside.

The worst thing you can do as a new Trader, is carried away with what seems like free money. If you use margin and your investment doesn't go the way you planned, then you end up with a large debt obligation for nothing. Ask yourself if you would buy stocks with your credit card. Of course, you wouldn't. Using margin excessively is essentially the same thing (though likely at a lower interest rate).

As a new investor, use margin sparingly, if at all. Use it only if you understand all its aspects and dangers. It can force you to sell all your positions at the bottom, the point at which you should be in the market for the big turnaround.

FOLLOWING THE HERD

Another common mistake made by new traders is that they blindly follow the herd, and as a result, they may either end up paying too much for hot stocks or may initiate short positions in securities that have already plunged and may be on the verge of turning around.

While experienced traders follow the dictum of "the trend is your friend," they are accustomed to exiting trades when they get too crowded. New traders, however, may stay in a trade long after the smart money has moved out of it. Novice traders may also lack the confidence to take a contrarian approach when required.

SHIRKING HOMEWORK

New traders are often guilty of not doing their homework or not conducting adequate research before initiating a trade. Doing homework is critical because beginner traders do not have the knowledge of seasonal trends, timing of data releases, and trading patterns that experienced traders possess. For a new trader, the urgency to put on a trade often overwhelms the need for undertaking some research, but this may ultimately result in an expensive lesson.

BUYING ON UNFOUNDED TIPS

Everyone probably makes this mistake at one point or another in their trading career. You may hear your relatives or friends talking about a stock that they heard will get bought out, have killer earnings or soon release a ground breaking new product. Even if these things are true, they do not necessarily mean that the stock is truly "the next big thing" and that you should rush onto your online brokerage account to place a buy order.

Other unfounded tips come from investment professionals on television and social media who often tout a specific stock as though it's a must-buy, but reality is nothing more than the flavor of the day.

This isn't to say that you should act at every stock tip. If one really grabs your attention, the first thing to do is consider the source. The next thing is to do your own homework. Make sure you "research, research and research some more" so that you know what you are buying and why.

TOO MUCH ATTENTION GIVEN TO FINANCIAL MEDIA

There is almost nothing on financial news shows that can help you achieve your goals. Turn them off. Think about it – if anyone really had profitable stock tips, trading advice or a secret formula to make a big profit, would they blab it on TV or sell it to you for Rs.200 per month? No – they'd keep their mouth shut, make their millions and not have to sell a newsletter to make a living.

Solution? Spend less time watching financial shows on TV and reading newsletters. Spend more time researching and other activities.

TRADING MULTIPLE MARKETS

Beginner traders may shift their focus from market to market, e.g., from stocks to options to currencies to commodity futures, to name a few. However, trading multiple markets can be a huge distraction and may prevent the novice trader from gaining the experience necessary to become a specialist and excel in one market.

OVERCONFIDENCE OR HUBRIS

Trading is a very demanding occupation, but the "beginner's luck" experienced by some novice traders may lead them to believe that trading is the proverbial road to quick riches. Such overconfidence is dangerous as it breeds complacency and encourages excessive risk-taking that may culminate in a trading disaster.

INEXPERIENCED DAY TRADING

If you insist on becoming an active trader, think twice before day trading. Day trading can be a dangerous game and should be attempted only by the most seasoned traders.

REMEMBER THE TAX AND DON'T IGNORE THE FEES

Keep in mind the tax consequences before you invest. You will get a tax break on some investments such as government bonds. Before you invest, look at what your return will be after adjusting for tax, taking into account the investment, your tax bracket, and your investment time horizon.

~~~
~~~

CHAPTER 4
Identify Your Erroneous Zones

To identify your erroneous zones as a Trader, you must ask yourself following question

Am I...

1. Trading based on Tips

2. Defining my risk before entering the Trade

3. Defining my entry point and my Target before entering.

4. Taking responsibility for the loss or blame the external factors

5. Executing the trade which I plan and not executing the trade which was not planned.

6. Following proper Money management in trading

7. Treating trading as a business.

8. Allotting time to learn trading as any other profession e.g. Engineering, Medical etc.

9. Having a system with a set of rules which needs to be always followed.

10. Doing the backtesting of the system to check whether it is offering any edge.

11. Keeping records of my trades

12. Making an effort consciously not to repeat the mistakes (a mistake means not following my rules)

13. Working on myself to improve/analyse

14. Reading enough books on trading (at least 1 in two months)

15. Attending any Paid seminar on Trading

Circle all the responses that are true for you. If you haven't circled at least 10 of the 15, you are not taking your trading seriously. Your financial health is in danger.

I will take you with me on this journey towards excellence but you have to promise me to give an honest effort towards learning the same.

~~~
~~~

SECTION B

Technical Analysis System

PART
One

Technical Analysis
Applicability

CHAPTER 5
Technical Analysis vs Fundamental Analysis

There are mainly two schools of thoughts to predict future Price of a stock. First is Fundamental Analysis and other is Technical analysis. I suggest you to make up your mind to follow Fundamental Analysis or Technical Analysis. In a nutshell, we can compare it as per the following:

	Fundamental Analysis (For Investing)	*Technical Analysis (For trading)*
Base Document	• Financial data such as Balance sheet, Cash flow, ROE, ROA etc • Industry trend • Competitor analysis • Economic outlook	• Price Movement (Charts) • Market Psychology

	Fundamental Analysis (For Investing)	*Technical Analysis (For trading)*
Time Horizon to attain the target	• Long term	• For long term, monthly and weekly charts are referred • For short term, daily and hourly charts are referred • For intraday, 3-minute to 5-minute charts are referred
Complexity	Not for everyone	• Easy to Learn • Easy to analyse

Why not to believe On Fundamental Analysis:

For carrying out the fundamental analysis of a stock, we need to refer many financial informations of the company which are in the public domain but:

- Can you confidently say that the information shared by companies are 100% correct or it is not manipulated?

- Do you have all insider information of a company such as a Merger, Acquisition, worker issues, change in management etc?

- Are you aware of the company's competitive strategy or their new products?

- Are you aware of any disruptive changes coming in the same Sector?

- Are you aware of Govt's change in policy affecting this company or its sector as a whole.?

There are many examples such as SATYAM, DHFL, YESBANK, RELCOM etc where companies were looking very sound but the price of these was going southward. It happened due to one or all of the above-listed reasons.

While, in Technical Analysis, we study the price pattern on charts. It means that if Price is changing (increasing or decreasing) due to any of the above-listed reasons, it will be visible on the charts and we can act accordingly.

~~~
~~~

CHAPTER 6
Technical Analysis - Basics

UNDERSTANDING GREED & FEAR

Market is mainly controlled by two emotions - Greed & Fear and these two emotions are Trader's worst enemy.

Fear creates Panic. Panic creates Supply, leading price to fall. Greed creates Exuberance, giving rise to demand which leads the price to rise.

Stock market is primarily a game of fear and Greed. Supply & Demand are by-products of these two emotions, battling it out for dominance in the market.

UNDERSTANDING BULL & BEAR

In very simple words, we can say that Bulls are those set of persons who take the price up and Bears are those sets of persons who bring the prices down or we can say Bulls expect the price to rise to get profit and Bears expect the price to fall to get profit.

Now the question is whether the same set of people always act as Bull or Bear. The answer is "No". You will be behaving as Bull if you are contributing & expecting the price to rise and you will be behaving as Bear if you are contributing & expecting the price to fall.

Next question comes in mind why price rise or why price falls? The reason is balance between demand & supply.

In other words, when there are more buyers than sellers, Price will rise. we will say that the Bulls are in control. Similarly, when there are more sellers than buyers, price will fall. we will say that Bears are in control.

ASSUMPTIONS IN TECHNICAL ANALYSIS

Technical Analysis is based on few key assumptions. One needs to be aware of these assumptions to ensure the best results.

1. The efficient market hypothesis (Markets discount everything)

This assumption tells us that, all known and unknown information in the public domain is reflected in the latest stock price. For example, there could be an insider of the company buying companies stock in large quantity in anticipation of good quarterly earning announcement while he does this secretely, the price reacts to the actions being taken by insider person or Smart money who are having better information than the general public. Thus, revealing to the technical analyst that this could be a good buy.

2. The 'how' is more important than 'why'

This is an extension to the first assumption. Going with the same example as discussed above – the technical analyst would not be interested in questioning **why** the insider bought the stock as long he knows **how** the price reacted to the insider's action.

3. Price moves in trend

All major moves in the market is an outcome of a trend. The concept of Trend is the foundation of technical analysis. For example, the recent upward movement in the NIFTY Index from 7937 to 11700 did not happen overnight. This move happened in a phased manner, in over 19 months i.e. from Jan'17 to Sep'18.

Another way to look at it is, once the trend is established, the price moves in the direction of the trend.

4. History tends to repeat itself

All human reacts similarly under similar circumstances. for example, when Stock price goes up, people get greedy and want to buy irrespective of the high price. Similarly, in a downtrend, people get fearful and want to sell irrespective of the low and unattractive prices. Due to it, the price tends to repeat itself over and over again.

~~~
~~~

CHAPTER 7
Charts & It's Constituents

As technical analysis is carried out through observation of charts, Hence, it is very important to understand various chart types, its constituents. Here, we will learn to read the charts.

Charts which are normally used in office meeting presentations do not offer much information for analysis of stock price projection. We need 4 data point to do a meaningful analysis.

Basically, there are three types of charts used by traders.

LINE CHARTS

The line chart is the most basic chart type and it uses only one data point to form the chart. When it comes to technical analysis, a line chart is formed by plotting the closing prices of a stock.

BAR CHART & JAPANESE CANDLESTICK CHARTS

Both of these charts provide 4 data point (Open, High, low, Close) on each tick. I suggest each beginner to use Candlestick charts as these provide more visual information showing green colour (or white) for a bullish day and red colour(or black) for a bearish day.

A BRIEF HISTORY OF JAPANESE CANDLE STICK CHARTS

It is worth to have a look at the history of Japanese candlestick charts. It will give you confidence that Traders are successfully using it for last 3 Centuries.

As the name suggests, the candlesticks originated from Japan. The earliest use of candlesticks dates back to the 18th century by a Japanese rice merchant named Homma Munehisa.

Though the candlesticks have been in existence for a long time in Japan, and are probably the oldest form of price analysis, the western world traders were clueless about it. It is believed that sometime around 1980's a trader named Steve Nison accidentally discovered candlesticks, and he actually introduced the methodology to the rest of the world.

Most of the pattern in candlesticks still retains the Japanese names; thus, giving an oriental feel to Technical analysis.

~~~
~~~

PART
Two

Candlesticks and Candlestick Patterns

CHAPTER 8
Anatomy of Candlestick

In a candlestick chart, candles can be classified as a bullish or bearish candle, usually represented by blue/green/white and red/black candles respectively. Needless to say, the colours can be customized to any colour of your choice; the technical analysis software allows you to do this. Here, we have opted for the white candle for the bullish and black candle for bearish candles.

Let us look at typical Candlestick. The candlestick, like a bar chart, is made of 3 components.

1. The Central real body – The real body, rectangular in shape connects the opening and closing price

2. Upper shadow – Connects the high point to the central real body

3. Lower Shadow – Connects the low point to central real body

Have a look at the following image to understand how a candlestick is formed:

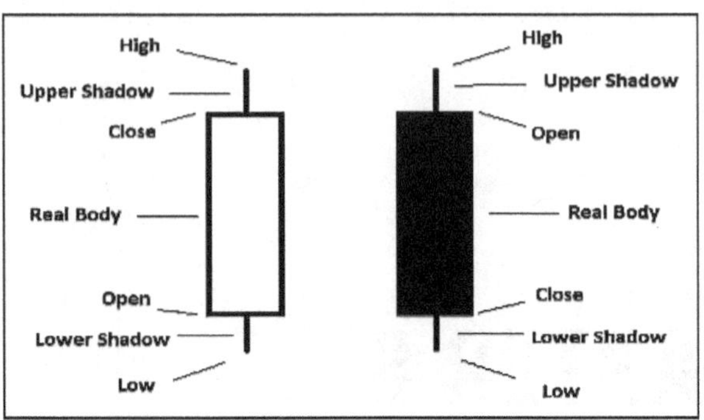

The open – When the markets open for trading, the first price at which a trade executes is called the opening Price.

The high – This represents the highest price at which the market participants were willing to transact for the given day.

The Low – This represents the lowest level at which the market participants were willing to transact for the given day.

The close – The Close price is the most important price because it is the final price at which the market closed for a particular period of time. The close serves as an indicator for the intraday strength. If the close is higher than the open, then it is considered a positive day and if the close is lower than the open it is considered a negative day.

Of course, we will deal with this in greater detail as we progress through to other chapters. The closing price also shows the market sentiment and serves as a reference point for the next day's trading. **For these reasons, the closing price is more important than the Open, High or Low prices.**

~~~
~~~

CHAPTER 9
Assumptions Specific to Candlesticks

Before we start dissection of Candlesticks and start learning about the patterns, there are few more assumptions that we need to keep in mind. These assumptions are specific to candlesticks. Please pay a lot of attention to these assumptions as you will need to apply it more often.

At this stage, these assumptions may not be very clear to you. I will explain them in greater detail as and when we proceed. However, do keep these assumptions in the back of your mind:

1. Buy strength and sell weakness

Strength is represented by a bullish candle (white) and weakness by a bearish (black) candle. Hence whenever you are buying ensure it is a white candle day and whenever you are selling, ensure it's a black candle day.

2. Be flexible with patterns (quantify and verify)

While the textbook definition of a pattern could state certain criteria, there could be minor variations to the pattern owing to market conditions. So, a bit of flexibility is always helpful. However, one needs to be flexible within limits, and hence it is required to always quantify the flexibility.

e.g. in case of Support & Resistance (you will learn it later), these will not be a simple trend line, instead, these will be a range.

3. Look for a prior trend

We always look for a reversal of the trend for entering in the trade. Hence, If you are looking at a bullish pattern, the prior trend should be bearish and likewise, if you are looking for a bearish pattern, the prior trend should be bullish.

~~~
~~~

CHAPTER 10
Validity of Candlestick Pattern Signal

Once we get a Bullish or Bearish signal from Candlestick Pattern, then next question comes upto what time period these signals remain valid.

As a thumb rule, it is valid for next 5-10 candle sticks of same time period candlestick.

It means that:

- A candlestick pattern signal is valid for next 5 to 10 months if you are referring monthly charts.

- A candlestick pattern signal is valid for next 5 to 10 weeks if you are referring weekly charts.

- A candlestick pattern signal is valid for next 5 to 10 days if you are referring daily charts.

- A candlestick pattern signal is valid for next 150 to 300 minutes (5 to 10 half hour candlesticks) if you are referring 30 min charts.

- A candlestick pattern signal is valid for next 25 to 50 minutes (5 to 10 candlesticks of 5 minutes) if you are referring 5 min charts.

- A candlestick pattern signal is valid for next 10 to 20 minutes (5 to 10 candlesticks of 2 minutes) if you are referring 2 min charts.

Please note that **validity of signal ends once you get opposite candlestick signal**.

~~~
~~~

CHAPTER 11
Time Frame and It's Application

A time frame is defined as the time duration during which one chooses to study a particular chart. In simple language, if you are using Monthly charts, it means each candle is representing Open, High, Low, Close (OHLC) of 1 month. Similarly, if you are using 5 min charts, it means that each candle is representing OHLC of 5 mint duration.

In charts provided by any broker, you will find Monthly, weekly, Daily or End of day (EOD), 4 hour, 1 hour, half hour, 10min, 5 min, 3 min & 1 min time frame charts.

In order to consistently make money in the markets, traders need to learn how to identify an underlying trend and trade around it accordingly. It is a famous quotation in the trading circle that "trade with the trend", and "the trend is your friend".

Trends can be classified as primary, intermediate and Short term. However, markets exist in several time frames simultaneously. As such, there can be conflicting trends within a particular stock depending on the time frame being considered. It is not out of the ordinary for a stock to be in a primary uptrend while being in downtrend in intermediate or short-term downtrend.

WHAT TIME FRAMES SHOULD YOU BE TRACKING?

A general rule is that the longer the time frame, the more reliable the signals being given. As you drill down in time frames, the charts become more polluted with false moves and noise.

Ideally, traders should use a longer time frame to define the primary trend of whatever they are trading.

Once the underlying trend is defined, traders can use their preferred time frame to define the intermediate trend and a faster time frame to define the short-term trend. Some examples of putting multiple time frames into use would be:

- A long-term Position Trader could hold the position for several weeks to Months. He could focus on weekly charts while using monthly charts to define the primary trend and daily charts to refine entries and exits.

- Swing trading involves holding a position either long or short at least overnight and or up to several weeks. The goal is to capture a larger price move that is not possible on an intra-day basis.

- Swing Trader focuses on daily charts for decisions, could use weekly charts to define the primary trend and 60-minute charts to define the short-term trend.

- A day trader could trade off of 5-minute charts, use 60-minute charts to define the primary trend and a 3-minute chart (or even a tick chart) to define the short-term trend.

The selection of what group of time frames to use is unique to each individual trader. Ideally, you should choose the main time frame you are interested in, and then choose a time frame above and below it, to complement the main time frame. **As such, you should be using the long-term chart to define the trend, the intermediate-term chart to provide the trading signal and the short-term chart to refine the entry and exit.**

Look at the following charts of Kotak Bank. It is a daily chart. Primary trend is clearly Uptrend, but Intermediate Trend is downtrend for 3-4 days around 21st May 18.

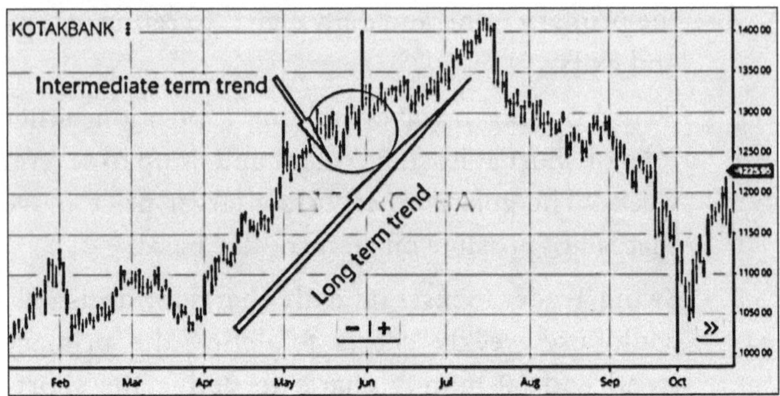

Now look at the following chart, it is 30min charts. On 21st May, again we can observe that price was initially going down, then went upward before going down again.

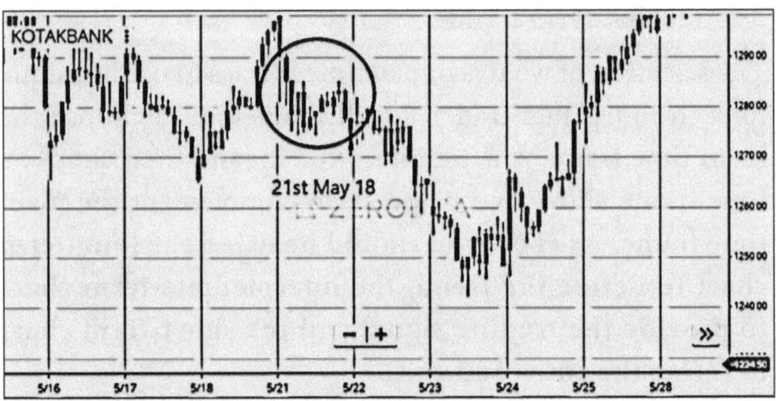


~~~
~~~

CHAPTER 12
Candlestick Patterns

In this topic, we will be learning various types of Candlestick Patterns. Instead of focussing on the fancy names of the patterns, I suggest you to focus on the undercurrent beneath each Pattern formation. Each pattern shows the battle between Bulls and Bears, Shifting of Power from Bulls to Bears or Bears to Bulls and their relative balance in the referred time frame.

BATTLE OF BULLS & BEARS

A candlestick depicts the battle between Bulls (buyers) and Bears (sellers) over a given period of time. An analogy to this battle can be made between two teams playing "Tug of War", which we can name as the Bulls and the Bears. The bottom half (low) of the candlestick represents a Team "Bears" and the top Half of Candlestick is representing the Team "Bulls"

If the Close is near high, Bulls were in more control than Bears i.e. the closer the close is to the high, the higher the control Bulls had over Bears.

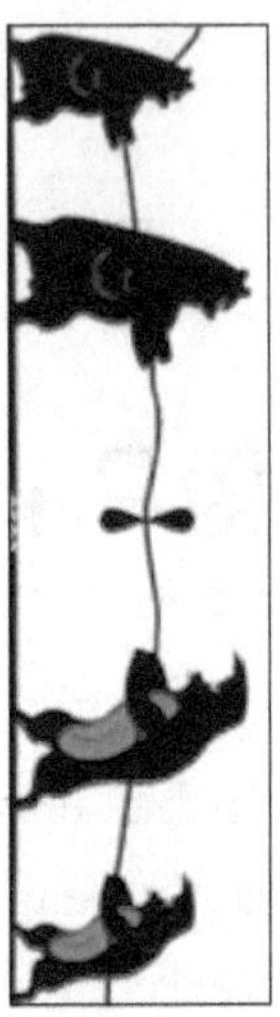

Similarly, the closer the close is to the Low, the higher the control Bears had over Bulls. While there are many variations, I have narrowed the field to 6 types of games (or candlesticks):

1. *Long white candlesticks* indicate that the **Bulls** controlled the game (trading) for most of the game.

2. *Long black candlesticks* indicate that the **Bears** controlled the game (trading) for most of the game.

3. *Small candlesticks* indicate that neither team could move the Rope and prices finished about where they started.

4. A *long lower shadow* indicates that the **Bears** controlled the ball for part of the game but lost

control by the end and the Bulls made an impressive comeback.

5. A *long upper shadow* indicates that the **Bulls** controlled the ball for part of the game but lost control by the end and the Bears made an impressive comeback.

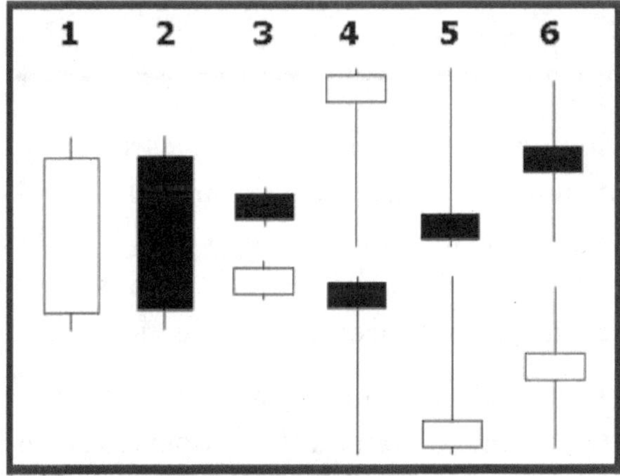

6. A *long upper and lower shadow* indicates that both the Bears and the Bulls had their moments during the game, but neither could put the other away, resulting in a standoff.

WHAT CANDLESTICK DO NOT TELL YOU

Candlesticks do not reflect the sequence of events between the open and close, only the relationship between the open and the close. The high and the low are obvious and indisputable, but candlesticks (and bar charts) cannot tell us which came first.

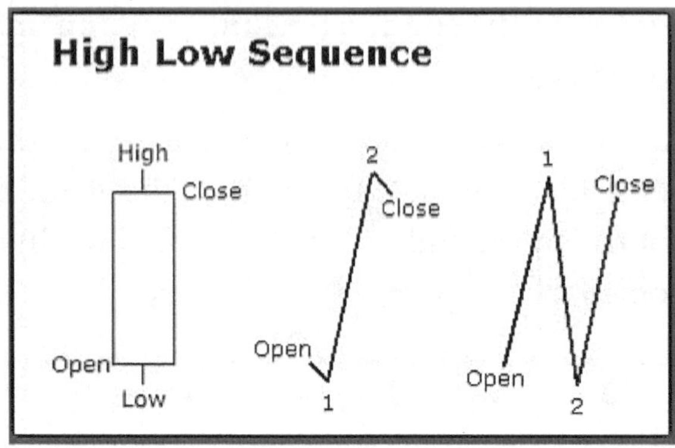

With a long white candlestick, the assumption is that prices advanced most of the session. However, based on the high/low sequence, the session could have been more volatile. The example above depicts two possible high/low sequences that would form the same candlestick.

The first sequence shows two small moves and one large move: a small decline off the open to form the low, a sharp advance to form the high, and a small decline to form the close.

The second sequence shows three rather sharp moves: a sharp advance off the open to form the high, a sharp decline to form the low, and a sharp advance to form the close.

The first sequence portrays strong, sustained buying pressure, and would be considered more bullish. The second sequence reflects more volatility and some selling pressure. These are just two examples, and there are hundreds of potential combinations that could result in the same candlestick. Inspite of this shortcoming,

Candlesticks still offer valuable information on the relative positions of the open, high, low and close. However, the trading activity that forms a particular candlestick, can vary.

LONG VS SHORT BODIES

Generally speaking, the longer the body is, the more intense the buying or selling pressure. Conversely, short candlesticks indicate little price movement and represent consolidation.

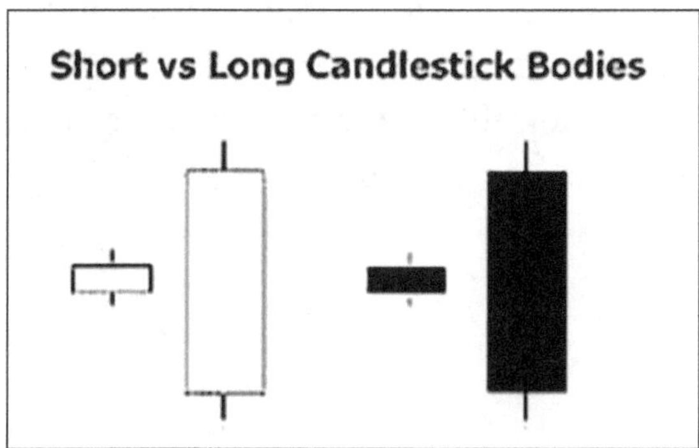

LONG WHITE CANDLESTICKS SHOW STRONG BUYING PRESSURE

The longer the white candlestick is, the further the close is above the open. This indicates that prices advanced significantly from open to close and buyers were aggressive.

While long white candlesticks are generally bullish, much depends on their position within the broader technical picture. After extended declines, long white candlesticks can mark a potential turning point or support level. If buying gets too aggressive after a long advance, it can lead to excessive bullishness.

LONG BLACK CANDLESTICKS SHOW STRONG SELLING PRESSURE

The longer the black candlestick is, the further the close is below the open. This indicates that prices declined significantly from the open and sellers were aggressive.

After a long advance, a long black candlestick can foreshadow a turning point or mark a future resistance level. After a long decline, a long black candlestick can indicate panic or capitulation.

~~~
~~~

CHAPTER 13
Single Candlestick Pattern

First, we will learn single candlestick pattern, then we will understand its use in a complete pattern.

13.1 MARUBOZU

In the Japanese language, The word Marubozu means "Bald" in Japanese. It indicates a stock has traded strongly in one direction throughout the session and closed at its high or low price of the day. A Marubozu candle is represented only by a body; it may have shadows extending from the top or bottom of the candle.

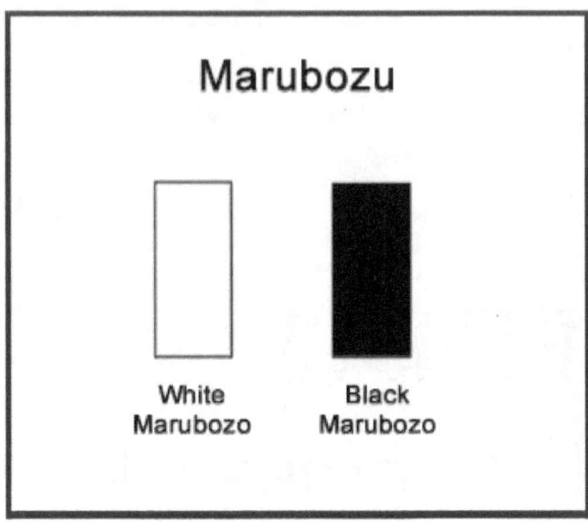

A white Marubozu candle has a long white body and is formed when the open equals the low and the close equals the high. The white Marubozu candle indicates that buyers controlled the price of the stock from the opening bell to the close of the day, and is considered very bullish.

A black Marubozu candle has a long black body and is formed when the open equals the high and the close equals the low. A black Marubozu indicates that sellers controlled the price from the opening bell to the close of the day, and is considered very bearish.

13.1.1 White Opening Marubozu

This candlestick represents extreme bullishness and it is characterized with a long white body that has an upper shadow but no lower shadow.

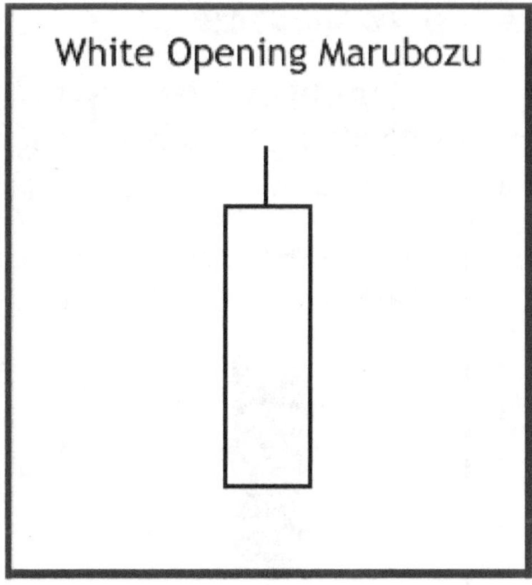

A White Opening Marubozu indicates that buyers controlled the price action from the first trade to the last trade. The day opens and prices continue to go up all day long without looking back, thus forming a long white day with no lower shadow. However, the day does not close at the high of the day, and thus creates an upper shadow.

The candlestick is generally bullish. However, its position within the broader technical picture is also important. It may show a potential turning point and that prices have reached a support level after an extended decline.

If it is seen after a long and significant rally, it may point to excessive bullishness, and that prices are at dangerously high levels.

13.1.2 Black Opening Marubozu

This candlestick represents extreme bearishness and it is characterized with a long black body that has a lower shadow but no upper shadow.

A Black Opening Marubozu indicates that the sellers controlled the price action from the first trade to the last trade. The day opens and prices continue to go down all day long without looking back, thus forming a long black day with no upper shadow. However, the day does not close at the low, and thus creates a lower shadow.

This candlestick is generally bearish. However, its position within the broader technical picture is also important. It may show a potential turning point and suggest that prices have reached to a resistance level after an extended rally.

If it is seen after a long decline, it may signal panic or capitulation, a final sell-off attempt before bulls regain control.

13.1.3 White Closing Marubozu

This candlestick represents extreme bullishness and it is characterized with a long white body that has a lower shadow but no upper shadow.

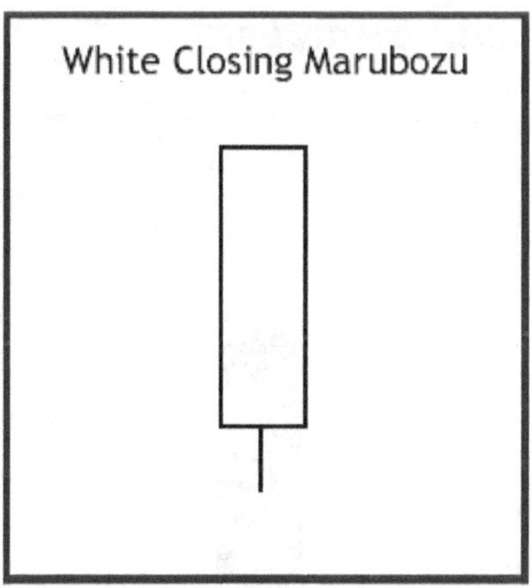

A White Closing Marubozu indicates that the buyers controlled the price action from the first trade to the last trade. The day opens and prices go slightly lower forming a lower shadow. This is followed by a rally that drives prices over the opening price, and the rally continues all day ending with a closing price equal to the high of the day. The bulls are very strong during the day except during the initial phase of the session.

This candlestick is generally bullish. However, its position within the broader technical picture is also important. It may show a potential turning point and suggests the fact that prices have reached a support level after an extended decline.

If it is seen after a long and significant rally, it may point to excessive bullishness, pointing that Price is dangerously high and it may be a final push by bulls before Bear regain control.

13.1.4 Black Closing Marubozu

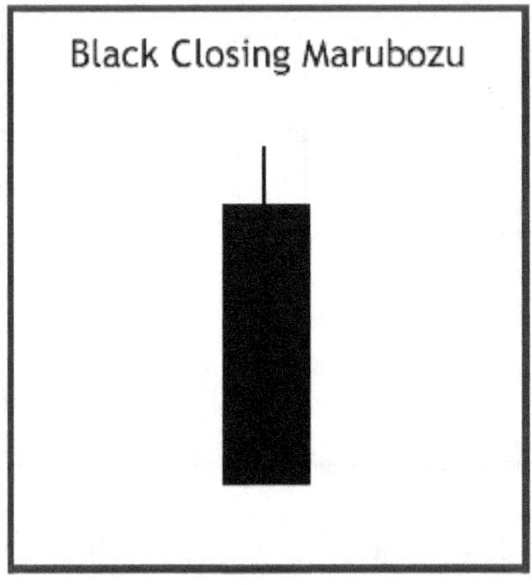

This candlestick represents extreme bearishness and it is characterized with a long black body that has an upper shadow but no lower shadow.

A Black Closing Marubozu indicates that sellers controlled the price action from the first trade to the last trade. The day opens and prices go slightly higher, forming an upper shadow. Then prices reverse direction moving below the opening level, and the decline continues all day ending with a closing price equal to the low of the day. The bears are very strong during the day except during the initial phase of the session.

The candlestick is generally bearish. However, its position within the broader technical picture is also important. It may show a potential turning point and that prices have reached a resistance level after an extended rally.

If it is seen after a long decline, it may signal panic or capitulation, a final sell-off attempt before bulls regain control.

13.2 DOJI

This candlestick is formed when the opening and closing prices are virtually equal.

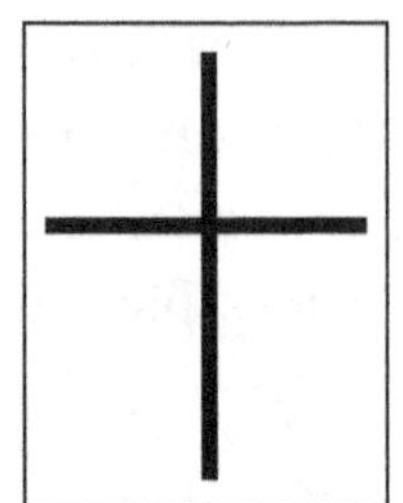

Ideally, the body should be colourless and have zero length. However, candlesticks with close-to-zero body lengths and white or black body colours are also accepted as Doji.

Doji is a particular signal showing indecision about the direction of the market and it represents a tug of war between buyers and sellers. It simply shows that prices have moved above and below the opening price during the day, but then the session closed either exactly at or very near the opening price. The overall result is a standoff.

It shows that neither the bulls nor the bears were able to gain control during the day and it is possible that a turning point could develop soon.

Doji is an important candlestick. It provides information on its own. It also features in other patterns as an important element. It needs to be interpreted in terms of a preceding trend or preceding candlesticks. The appearance of a Doji after an advance or a long white candlestick signals that buying pressure is getting weaker.

Its appearance after a decline or a long black candlestick signals that selling pressure is diminishing. Essentially, Doji gives the message that the forces of supply and demand are becoming more evenly matched and consequently a change in trend may be near.

13.2.1 Umbrella Doji (or Dragonfly Doji)

This candlestick is a type of Doji characterized with no upper shadow but a long lower shadow. It is also known as the Dragonfly Doji.

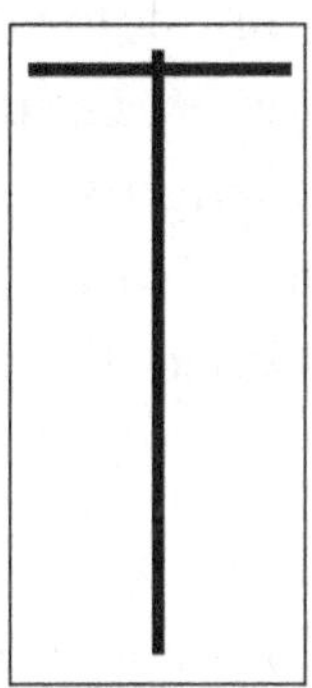

Ideally, the body should be colourless and have zero length. However, candlesticks with close-to-zero body lengths and white or black body colours are also acceptable. Only the lower shadow exists and it is long.

The Umbrella indicates that sellers mostly dominated trading during the day and they were able to drive prices lower. However, buyers resurfaced at the end of the day and they successfully pushed prices back to the opening level and to the day's high.

The Umbrella has the potential to signal a bullish reversal at the bottom if it appears after a long downtrend, long black candlestick or if it is seen at a support level.

Likewise, umbrella may signal a bearish reversal at the top if it appears after a long uptrend, a long white candlestick or if it is seen at a resistance level.

13.2.2 Inverted Umbrella Doji (Gravestone Doji)

This candlestick is a type of Doji characterized with no lower shadow but a long upper shadow. It is also known as the Gravestone Doji.

The body should be colorless and have zero length. However, candlesticks with close-to-zero body lengths and white or black body colors are also acceptable. Only the upper shadow exists and it is long.

The Inverted Umbrella indicates that buyers dominated trading and they were able to drive prices higher during the day. However, sellers resurfaced by the end of the day and pushed prices back to the opening price level and to the day's low.

The Inverted Umbrella has the potential to point out evidence for buying pressure and indicate a potential bullish reversal if it appears after a long downtrend, long black candlestick or if it is seen at a support level.

Likewise, it may show a failed rally and indicate a potential bearish reversal if it appears after a long uptrend, long white candlestick or if it is seen at a resistance level.

13.3 SPINNING TOP

This candlestick has a tiny white body with upper and lower shadows that have a greater length than the body. It is accepted as a type of Doji and will act as a Doji when it appears

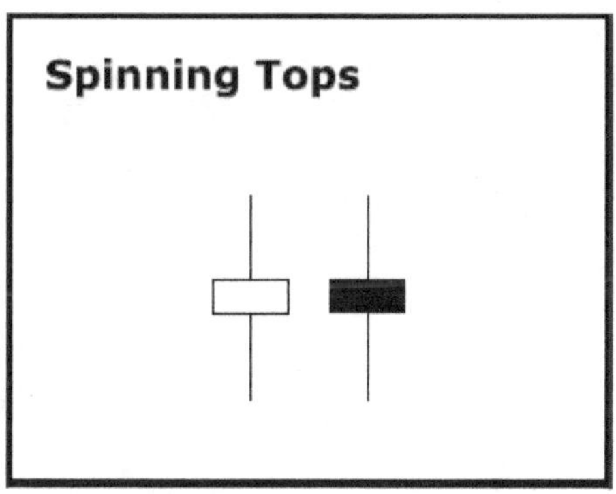

The market moves higher and then sharply lower, or vice versa. It then closes near the opening price creating a tiny body. This represents complete indecision between the bulls and the bears. The actual length of the shadows is not important. The small body relative to the shadows is what makes the spinning top.

If a Spinning Top is observed after a long rally or a long white candlestick, this implies weakness among the bulls and it is a warning of a potential change or an interruption in the trend.

If a Spinning Top is observed after a long decline or a long black candlestick, this implies weakness among the bears and it is a warning of a potential change or an interruption in the trend.

Like most other single candlestick patterns, the Spinning Top has low reliability. It reflects only one day's trading and can be interpreted both as a continuation or a reversal pattern. This candlestick needs to be used with other candlesticks to confirm a trend.

13.4 BULLISH HAMMER

This pattern occurs at the bottom of a trend or during a downtrend and it is called a Hammer since it is hammering out of a bottom. It is a single candlestick pattern that has a long lower shadow and a small body at or very near the top of its daily trading range.

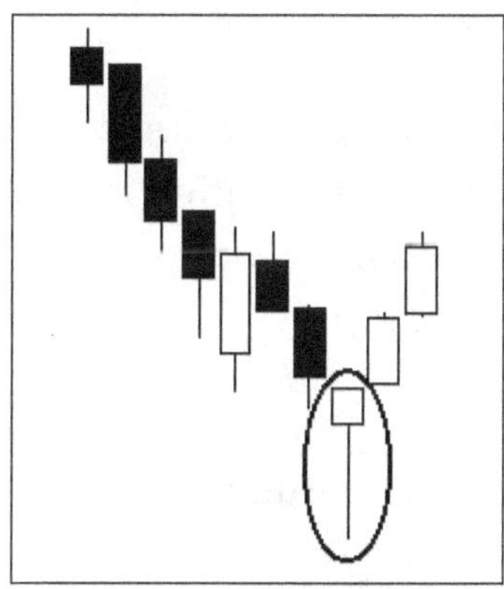

Pattern Requirements and Flexibility

The body of the Hammer should be small. The lower shadow should be at least twice as long as the body, but not shorter than an average candlestick. It is desired that there is no or a very tiny upper shadow. The bottom of the Hammer's body should be lower than both of the two preceding black candlesticks.

How to interpret

The Bullish Hammer appears in a downtrend and it sells off sharply following the market open. After the decline ceases, the market almost returns to the high of the day. Apparently, the market fails to continue on the selling side. This observation reduces the previous bearish sentiment causing Bears to feel increasingly uneasy with their positions. If the body of the Hammer is white, then the situation looks even better for the Bulls.

Entry

The confirmation level is defined as the top of the Hammer's body. Buy confirmation is triggered once Prices crosses above this level.

Stop Loss

The stop loss level is defined as the low of the Bullish Hammer shadow.

13.5 BEARISH HANGING MAN

The pattern occurs at the top of a trend or during an uptrend. The name Hanging Man comes from the fact that the candlestick looks somewhat like a hanging man. It is a single candlestick pattern that has a long lower shadow and a small body at or very near the top of its daily trading range.

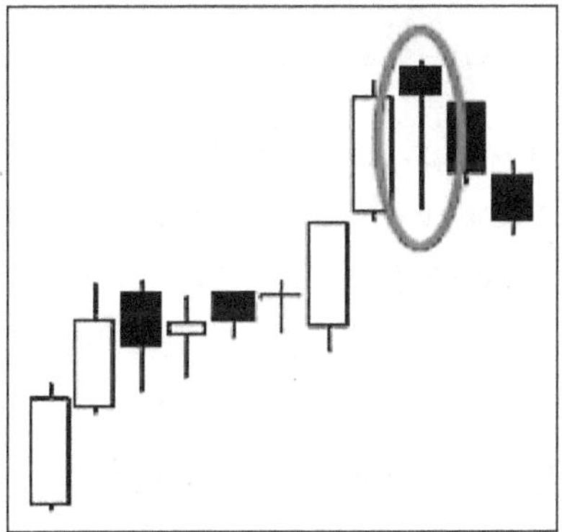

Pattern Requirements and Flexibility

The body of the Hanging Man should be small. The lower shadow should be at least twice as long as the body, but not shorter than an average candlestick. It is desired that the upper shadow is very small, or better nil. The top of the Hanging Man's body should be above both of the two preceding white candlesticks.

How to interpret

The Hanging Man is a bearish reversal pattern. It signals a market top or a resistance level. Since it is seen after an advance, it signals that the balance of power is shifting towards Bears. The long lower shadow indicates that the Bears pushed prices lower during the session. Even though the Bulls regained their footing and drove prices higher by the finish, Bulls clearly felt the warning signal. If the body is black, it shows that the close was not able to get back to the opening price level, which has potentially more bearish implications.

Entry

The confirmation level is defined as the midpoint of Hanging Man's lower shadow. Prices should cross below this level for confirmation.

Stop Loss

The stop loss level is defined as the high of the Hanging Man.

13.6 BULLISH INVERTED HAMMER

This pattern consists of a black body followed by an Inverted Hammer that is characterized by a long upper shadow and a small body. It is similar in shape to the Bearish Shooting Star but unlike the Shooting Star, the Inverted Hammer appears in a downtrend and signals a bullish reversal.

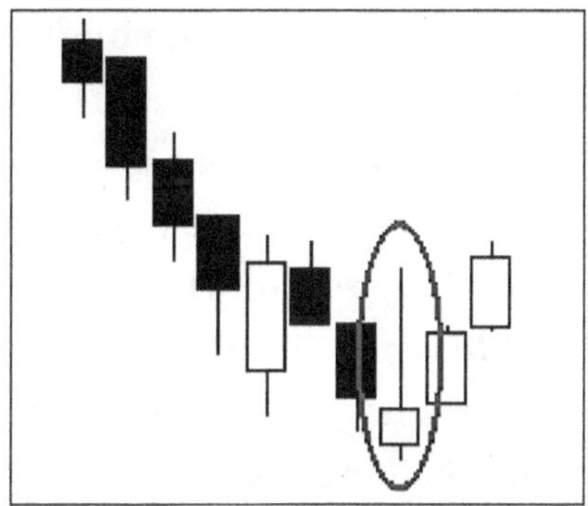

Pattern Requirements and Flexibility

The body of the Inverted Hammer should be small. The upper shadow should be at least twice as long as the body but not shorter than an average candlestick length. It is desired that there is no or a very tiny lower shadow. The bottom of the inverted hammer should be lower than the preceding candlestick's body.

How to interpret

The pattern occurs in a bearish background and the black candlestick that appears on the first day further supports the bearishness. On the second day, in which an Inverted

Hammer is seen, market opens below the previous close giving comfort to Bears. Then prices change direction and we see a rally. However, the bulls do not succeed in sustaining the rally during the rest of the day and prices finally close either at or near the low of the day.

At this point. It may not be clear why this type of price action is interpreted as a potential reversal signal. The answer has to do with what happens over the next day. If the next day opens above the body of the Inverted Hammer, it means that those who shorted at the opening or closing of the Inverted Hammer day are losing money. The longer the market holds above the Inverted Hammer's body, the more likely these shorts will attempt to cover their positions. This may ignite a rally as a result of covered short positions, which may then inspire the bottom pickers to take long positions.

Entry

The confirmation level is defined as the midpoint of the upper shadow of the inverted hammer. Prices should cross above this level for confirmation.

Stop Loss

The stop loss level is defined as the low of the Inverted Hammer.

13.7 BEARISH SHOOTING STAR

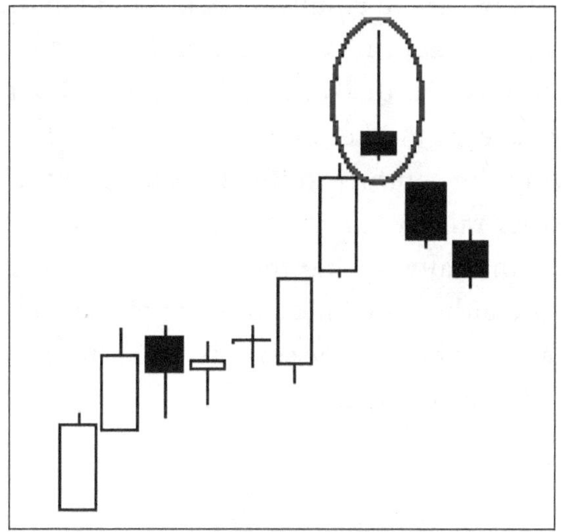

This pattern consists of a white body followed by an Inverted Hammer that is characterized by a long upper shadow and a small body. It is similar in shape to the Bullish Inverted Hammer pattern but unlike it, the Shooting Star appears in an uptrend and signals a bearish reversal.

Pattern Requirements and Flexibility

The body of the Inverted Hammer should be small. The upper shadow must be at least twice as long as the body but not shorter than an average candlestick length. It is desired that there is no or a very tiny lower shadow. The top of the Inverted Hammer's body should be higher than the preceding candlestick's body.

How to interpret

The pattern occurs in a bullish background and the white candlestick that appears on the first day further supports the bullishness. On the second day, in which an Inverted Hammer is seen, market opens higher than the previous close giving the comfort to Bulls. Adding to the comfort. Price further rallies. However, the bulls do not succeed in sustaining the rally during the rest of the day and prices finally close either at or near the low of the day. Bulls are now uneasy and have some serious concern about holding their profitable positions.

Entry

The confirmation level is defined as the low of the Inverted Hammer's body. Prices should cross below this level for confirmation.

Stop Loss

The stop loss level is defined as high of shooting star.

13.8 BULLISH BELT HOLD

Bullish Belt Hold is a single candlestick pattern. Basically, a White Opening Marubozu that occurs in a downtrend. It opens on gap down and then a rally begins during the day against the overall trend of the market, which eventually stops with a close near the high, leaving a small shadow on top of the candle.

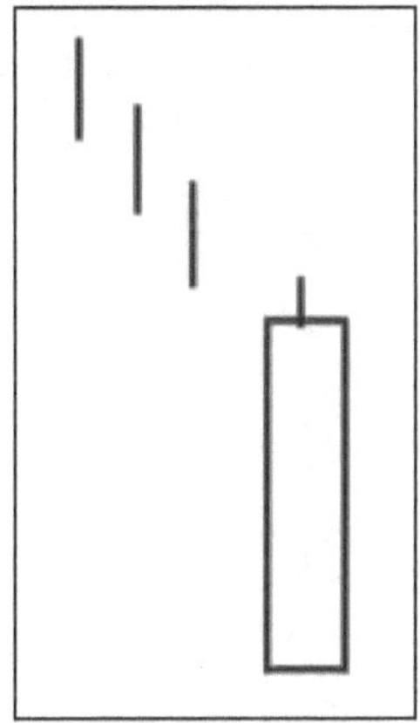

How to interpret

The market opens lower with a significant gap in the direction of the prevailing downtrend. So, the first impression reflected in the opening price is the continuation of the downtrend and strongness of Bears. However, after the market opening, things change rapidly and Bulls take control and keep their control until close of the day. This causes much concern among the Bears, leading to the covering of their Short positions, which could reverse the direction of the trend and start a rally for the bulls.

Entry

The confirmation level is defined as the close of Marubozu. Prices should cross above this level for confirmation.

Stop Loss

The stop loss level is defined as the low of the Marubozu.

13.9 BEARISH BELT HOLD

Bearish Belt Hold is a single candlestick pattern, basically, a Black Opening Marubozu that occurs in an uptrend. It opens Gap up, and then prices begin to fall during the day against the overall trend of the market, which eventually stops with a close near the low, leaving a small shadow at the bottom of the candle.

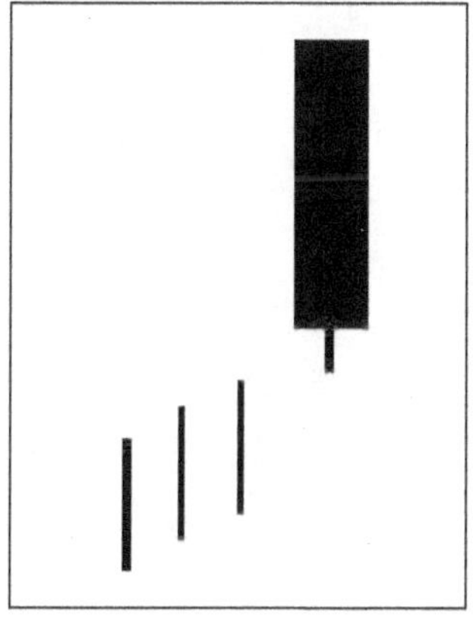

How to Interpret

The market opens higher, with a significant gap in the direction of the prevailing uptrend. So, the first impression reflected in the opening price is the continuation of the uptrend and strong control of Bulls over Bears. However, after the market opening, things change rapidly. Bears takes Control until the close of the day. The market moves in the opposite direction from there on. This causes much concern among the bulls, leading them to cover their Bullish positions, which could reverse the direction of the trend and start a sell-off.

Entry

The confirmation level is defined as the last close. Prices should cross below this level for confirmation.

Stop Loss

The stop loss level is defined as the high of the Marubozu Candlestick.

~~~
~~~

CHAPTER 14
Multi Candlestick Pattern

In this topic, we will learn about patterns which are formed taking into consideration of two or more Candlesticks.

14.1 BULLISH ENGULFING PATTERN

This pattern is characterized by a large white body engulfing a preceding smaller black body, which appears during a downtrend. The white body does not necessarily engulf the shadows of the black body but totally engulfs the body itself. This is an important bottom reversal signal.

- The market is characterized by a prevailing downtrend.
- A black body is observed on the first day.

- The white body that is formed on the second day completely engulfs the black body of the preceding day.

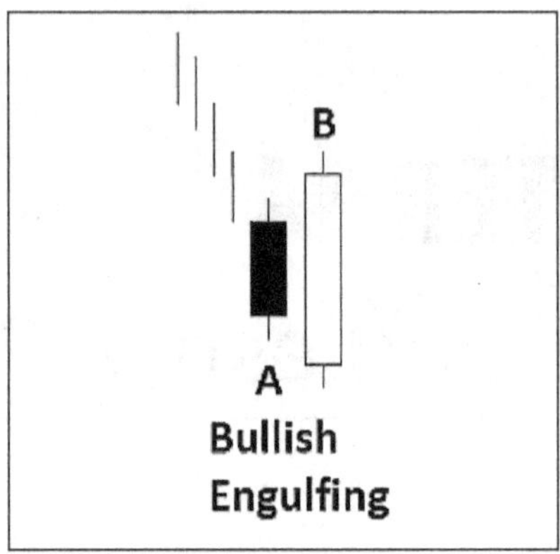

Pattern Requirements and Flexibility

The length of the first black candlestick in Bullish Engulfing is not important. It can even be a Doji. However, the second one has to be a normal or long white candlestick. Either the body tops or the body bottoms of the two candlesticks may be at the same level, but in any case, the white body should be longer than the previous black body.

How to Interpret

While the market is characterized by a downtrend, a lower volume of selling is observed with the occurrence of a black body on the first day. The next day, the market opens at new lows which make Bear comfortable. It looks as if there's going to be more bearish trading, however, the downtrend loses momentum and the Bulls take the lead during the day. The buying pressure overcomes selling and finally, the market closes above the open of the previous day. The downtrend is damaged.

Entry

The confirmation level is defined as the last close. Prices should cross above this level for confirmation.

Stop Loss

The stop loss level is defined as the low of the Engulfing Candlestick

14.2 BEARISH ENGULFING PATTERN

This pattern is characterized by a large black body engulfing a preceding smaller white body, which appears during an uptrend. The black body does not necessarily engulf the shadows of the white body but totally engulfs the body itself. This is an important top reversal signal.

- The market is characterized by a prevailing uptrend.

- A white body is formed observed on the first day.

- The black body that is formed on the second day completely engulfs the white body of the preceding day.

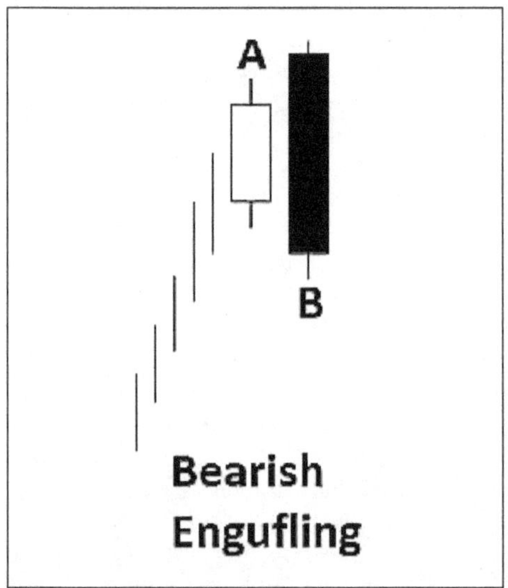

Pattern Requirements and Flexibility

The length of the first white candlestick is not important. It can even be a Doji. The second one, however, has to be a normal or long black candlestick. Either the body tops or the body bottoms of the two candlesticks may be at the same level, but in any case, the black body of the Bearish Engulfing Pattern should be longer than the previous white body.

How to Interpret

While the market is characterized by a definite uptrend, lower volume of buying is observed with the occurrence of a white body on the first day. The next day, the market opens at new highs. It looks as if Bulls are in total control however, the uptrend loses momentum and the Bears take the lead during the day. The selling pressure overcomes buying and finally, the market closes below the open of the previous day. The uptrend is damaged.

Entry

The confirmation level is defined as the last close. Prices should cross below this level for confirmation.

Stop loss

The stop loss level is defined as the high of the Engulfing Candlestick.

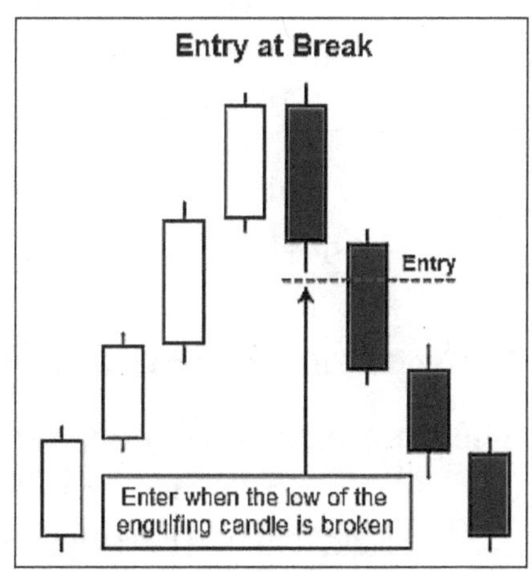

14.3 BULLISH HARAMI

This pattern consists of a black body and a small white body that is completely inside the range of the black body. If an outline is drawn for the pattern, it looks like a pregnant woman. This is not a coincidence. "Harami" is an old Japanese word for "pregnant". The black candlestick is "the mother" and the small candlestick is "the baby".

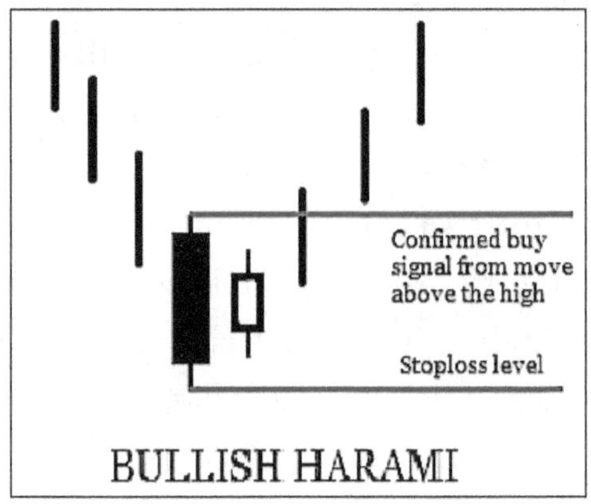

BULLISH HARAMI

- The market is characterized by a prevailing downtrend.
- A black body is observed on the first day.
- The white body that is formed on the second day is completely engulfed by the body of the first day.

Pattern Requirements and Flexibility

The pattern consists of two candlesticks, in which the first day's black candlestick engulfs the following day's white candlestick. The first one has to be a normal or long black candlestick. Either the second candlestick is near top of first candlestick or near bottom of the first candlestick or both may be at the same level, but whatever the case, the white body should be smaller than the previous black body.

How to interpret

The Bullish Harami is a sign of disparity in the market's health. The market is characterized by a downtrend under strong Control of Bears and there is heavy selling reflected by a black Candlestick, which further supports the bearishness. However, the next day prices open higher or at the close of the preceding day and the Bears are alarmed. This leads to the covering of many short positions, causing the price to rise further. The latecomers short the trend they missed the first time, and slow down the rise. Thus, a small white body is formed. This may signal a trend reversal since the second day's small real body shows that the bearish power is diminishing and Bulls are gaining control.

Entry

The confirmation level is highest of the both candles.

Stop Loss

The stop loss level is defined as the lower of the lows of last two Candlesticks.

14.4 BEARISH HARAMI

This pattern consists of a white body and a small black body that is completely inside the range of the white body. If an outline is drawn for the pattern, it looks like a pregnant woman. This is not a coincidence. "Harami" is an old Japanese word for "pregnant". The white candlestick is "the mother" and the small candlestick is "the baby".

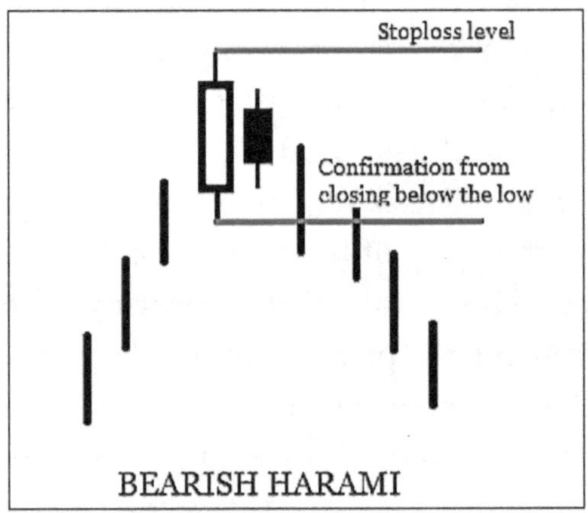

- The market is characterized by a prevailing uptrend.
- A white body is observed on the first day.
- The black body that is formed on the second day is completely engulfed by the body of the first day.

Pattern Requirements and Flexibility

The pattern consists of two candlesticks, in which the first day's white candlestick engulfs the following day's black candlestick. The first one should be a normal or a long white candlestick. Either the second candlestick is near top of first candlestick or near bottom of the first candlestick or both may be at the same level, but whatever the case, the black body should be smaller than the previous white body.

How to Interpret

The Bearish Harami is a sign of disparity in the market's health. The market is characterized by an uptrend and a bullish mood, and there is heavy buying indicated by a white body, which shows that Bulls are in full Control. However, the next day prices open lower or at the close of the preceding day and stay in a small range throughout the day, closing even lower, but still within the previous day's body. Bulls are now concerned about the strength of the market due to this suddenly deteriorating trend.

Entry

Lowest of the last two Candles. Prices should cross below this level for confirmation.

Stop Loss

The stop loss level is defined as the higher of the last two highs.

14.5 BULLISH PIERCING PATTERN

This is a bottom reversal pattern with two candlesticks. A black candlestick appears on the first day while a downtrend is in progress. The second day opens at a new low, with a gap down and closes more than halfway into the prior black body, leading to the formation of a strong white candlestick.

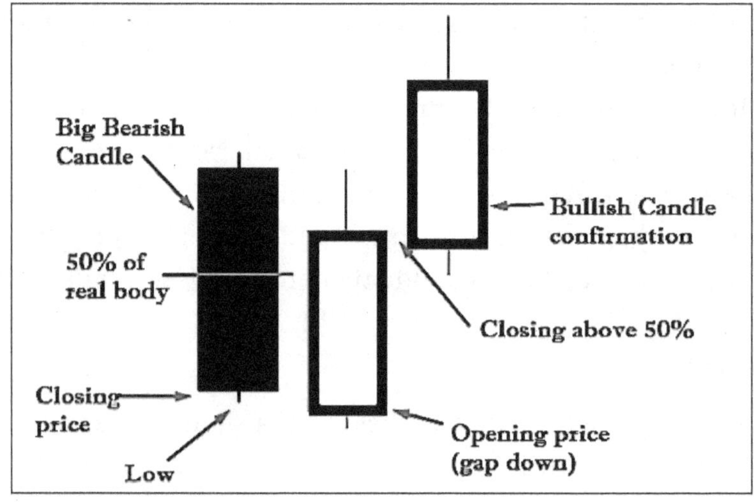

- The market is characterized by a prevailing downtrend.

- A black candlestick appears on the first day.

- A white candlestick opens on the second day with a gap down and closes more than halfway into the body of the first day.

- The second day fails to close above the body of the first day.

Pattern Requirements and Flexibility

The first day of the Bullish Piercing Line pattern is a normal or long black candlestick. The second day should open well below the close of the first day and close more than halfway into the prior black candlestick's body. However, the close of the second day must stay inside the body of the first day.

How to interpret

The market moves in a downtrend. Bears are in complete control. The first black body reinforces this view. The next day the market opens lower via a gap, showing that the Bears are still in Control. After this very bearish open, bulls decide to take the lead. The market surges toward the close, prices start to go up resulting in a close way above the previous day's close. Now the bears are losing their confidence and are re-evaluating their short positions. The potential buyers start thinking that new lows may not hold and perhaps it is time to take long positions.

Entry

The confirmation level is defined as the last close. Prices should cross above this level for confirmation.

Stop Loss

The stop loss level is defined as the last low.

14.6 BEARISH BLACK CLOUD COVER

This is a top reversal pattern with two candlesticks. A white candlestick appears on the first day while an uptrend is in progress. The second day opens at a new high, with a gap up and closes more than halfway into the prior white body, leading to the formation of a strong black candlestick.

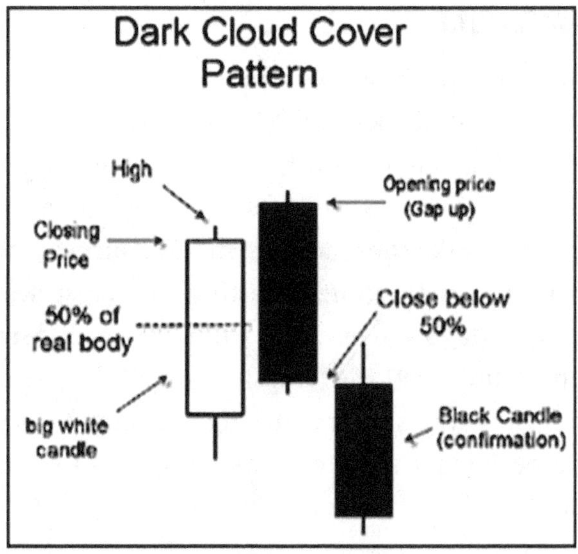

- The market is characterized by a prevailing uptrend.

- A white candlestick appears on the first day.

- A black candlestick opens on the second day with a gap up and closes more than halfway into the body of the first day.

- The second day fails to close below the body of the first day.

Pattern Requirements and Flexibility

The first day of the Bearish Dark Cloud Cover pattern is a normal or long white candlestick. The second day should open well above the close of the first day and close more than halfway into the prior white candlestick's body. However, the close of the second day must stay inside the body of the first day.

How to interpret

The market moves in an uptrend showing that Bulls are in control. The first white body reinforces this view. The next day the market opens higher via a gap, showing that the Bulls are still in full control. After this very bullish open, Bears decide to take the lead. The market plunges toward the close, prices start to go down resulting in a close way below the previous day's close. Now the Bulls are losing their confidence and are re-evaluating their long positions. The potential short sellers start thinking that new highs may not hold and perhaps it is time to take short positions.

Entry

The confirmation level is defined as the last close. Prices should cross below this level for confirmation.

Stop Loss

The stop loss level is defined as the last high.

14.7 BULLISH MORNING STAR

This is a three-candlestick pattern signalling a major bottom reversal. It is composed of a black candlestick followed by a short candlestick, which characteristically gaps down to form a Star. Then we have a third white candlestick whose closing is well into the first session's black body. This is a meaningful bottom pattern.

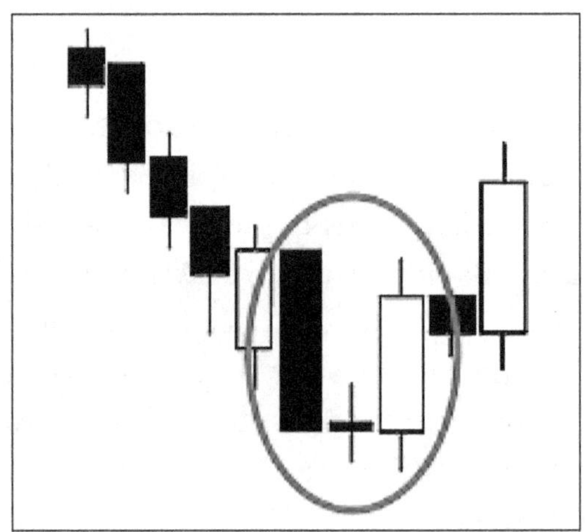

How to recognise

- The market is characterized by a prevailing downtrend.

- We see a black candlestick on the first day.

- On second day, we see a short candlestick that gaps in the direction of the downtrend.

- A white candlestick is observed on the third day should open at or higher of day 2 candlestick

- The third day's closing must reach the midpoint between the first day's opening and the second day's lowest body level.

How to interpret

A downtrend is in progress and Bears are in complete control. The black candlestick confirms the continuation of the downtrend. On second day, The appearance of the short candlestick that causes a gap indicates that Bears are still pushing down the price. However, Bulls and Bears are in balance as candle is a doji or a Spinning top. The third day is a white body showing that Bulls are in Control that moves into the first day's black body. A significant trend reversal has occurred.

Entry

The confirmation level is defined as the last close. Prices should cross above this level for confirmation.

Stop Loss

The stop loss level is defined as the lower of the last two lows.

14.8 BEARISH EVENING STAR

This is a three-candlestick pattern signalling a major top reversal. It is composed of a white candlestick followed by a short candlestick, which characteristically gaps up to form a star. Then we have a third black candlestick whose closing is well into the first session's white body. This is a meaningful top pattern.

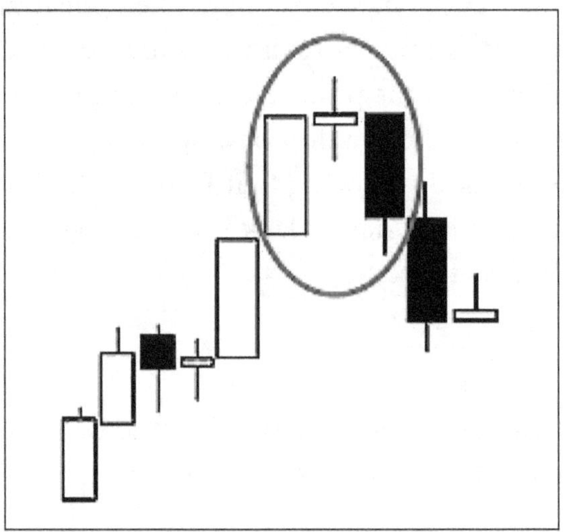

How to recognise

- The market is characterized by a prevailing uptrend.

- We see a white candlestick on the first day.

- On the second day, we see a short candlestick (white or black) that gaps in the direction of the uptrend.

- A black candlestick is observed on the third day should open at or lower than the highest level of the body of the second candlestick

- The third day's closing must reach the midpoint between the first day's opening and the second day's highest body level.

How to interpret

An uptrend is being observed and Bulls are in full Control. The white candlestick confirms the continuation of the uptrend. The appearance of the short candlestick that makes a gap indicates that bulls are still pushing up the price. However, the tight price action on the second day between the open and the close shows that Bulls and Bears are in balance indicating indecision. The third day is a black body that moves into the first day's white body. A significant trend reversal has occurred.

Entry

The confirmation level is defined as the last close. Prices should cross below this level for confirmation.

Stop Loss

The stop loss level is defined as the higher of the last two highs.

14.9 TWEEZER TOPS & TWEEZER BOTTOMS

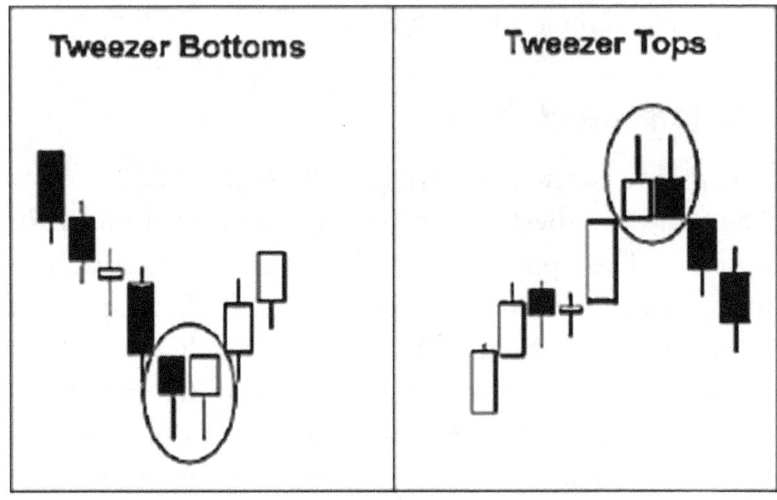

Tweezers are both a topping and bottoming pattern – patterns that indicate a shift in trend direction – although a broader context is usually needed to confirm the signal since tweezers can occur frequently.

A topping pattern occurs when the highs of two candlesticks occur at almost exactly the same level following an advance.

A bottoming pattern occurs when the lows of two candlesticks occur at almost exactly the same level following a decline.

Additional criteria are that the first candle has a large real body (difference between open and close), but the second candle can be pretty much of any size; therefore, the two candles may look quite different. For example, in a tweezers top, the first candlestick may be a very strong up candle, closing near the high, while the second candle may be a doji, that doesn't close near the high but still has a similar high to the first candle.

The premise behind this being a topping or bottoming pattern is that the first candle shows a strong move in the current direction, while the second candle pauses or even completely reverses the prior days' price action. A short-term shift in momentum has occurred, which traders should be aware of.

Hot to Trade Tweezers

Candlestick patterns can occur frequently in financial markets, and tweezers are no exception. Based on overall conditions, their appearance can be benign or trade worthy.

If an overall trend is in place, when tweezers occur during a pullback, it signals a potential entry point, as the pattern indicates that the pullback is over and the price is likely to move in the trending direction again. By using tweezers in this manner – entering on pullbacks in alignment with the overall trend – the success rate for these patterns improves.

Tweezers do not provide a profit target, so the target must be based on other factors, such as the trend and overall momentum.

Stop Loss

- For a bottom pattern, a stop loss can be placed below the tweezers' lows.

- For a topping pattern, the stop can be placed above the tweezers' highs.

~~~
~~~

CHAPTER 15
Blending Candlesticks

Suppose you are looking at 15 minutes chart and found there is a Bullish Engulfing Pattern. You now shifted to 30minutes chart and to your surprise, there is no Bullish Engulfing Pattern present instead you found a Hammer.

Same way, if you are looking at Daily charts and found some patterns and on observing Weekly charts, you found different patterns.

You may be doubting whether your charting software is working properly or not. Let me assure you it is working fine. Charts which you are observing on different time frame are correct and what you are observing is due to blending of candlesticks.

Candlestick patterns are made up of one or more candlesticks and can be blended together to form one candlestick. This blended candlestick captures the essence of the pattern and can be formed using the following:

- The open of the first candlestick

- The close of the Second candlestick

- The high and low of the pattern

Please go through the following example and understand it carefully.

Candlesticks 1	Candlesticks 2	Blended Candlestick 3 = 1+2	Remark
Open = 430	Open= 426	Open = 430	Open of 1
High = 445	High = 460	High = 460	Highest of 1 & 2
Low = 415	Low = 420	Low = 415	Lowest of 1 & 2
Close = 425	Close= 450	Close= 450	Close of 2

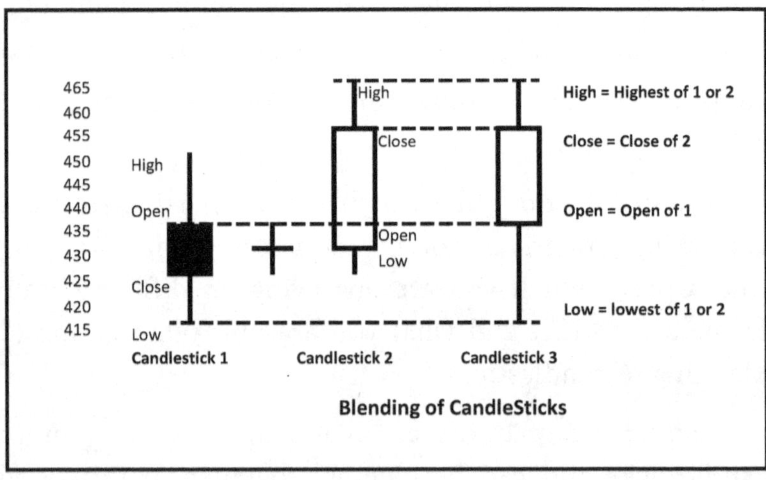

Blending of CandleSticks

RULE FOR BLENDING CANDLESTICKS

Now Blended Candlesticks of time frame T =

Candlesticks 1 of Time frame T1 + Candlesticks 2 of Time frame T2

Where T = T1 + T2

   Open = Open of Candlesticks 1

   Close = Close of Candlesticks 2

   High = Highest of Candlesticks 1 or Candlesticks 2

   Low = Lowest of Candlesticks 1 or Candlesticks 2

Please go through the following example and understand it carefully.

- A Bullish Engulfing Pattern blends into a Hammer.
- A Bearish Engulfing Pattern blends into a Shooting Star

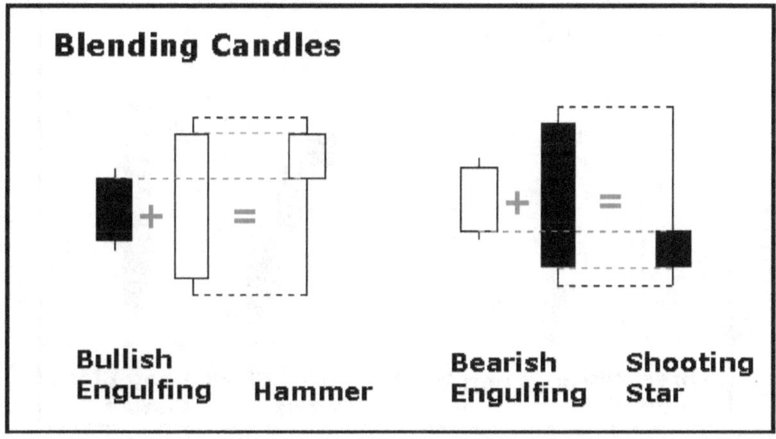

- A Piercing Pattern blends into a Hammer.

- A Dark Cloud Cover Pattern creates a Shooting Star.

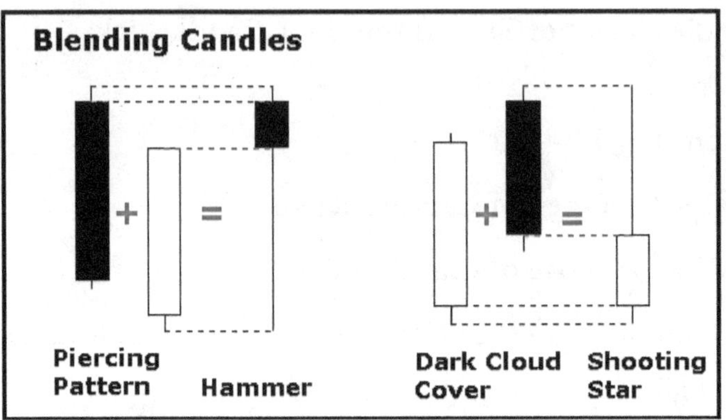

More than two candlesticks can be blended using the same guidelines: open from the first, close from the last and high/low of the pattern. Blending Three White Soldiers creates a long white candlestick and blending Three Black Crows creates a long black candlestick.

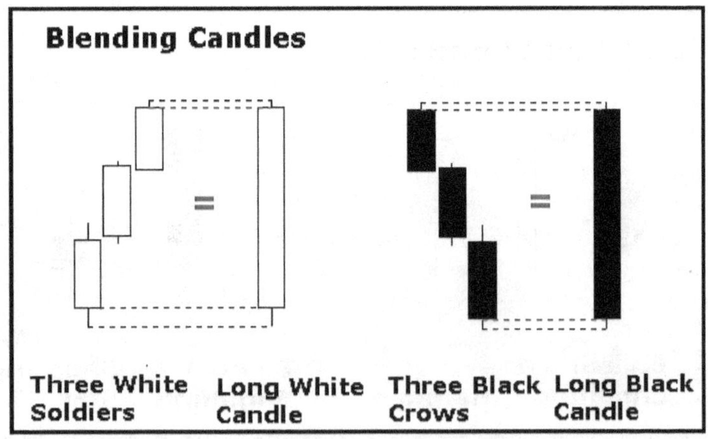


~~~
~~~

PART
Three

Technical Indicators

CHAPTER 16
Trend Lines

Technical analysis is built on the assumption that prices moves in trend. Trend Lines are an important tool in technical analysis for both trend identification and confirmation.

A trend line is a straight line that connects two or more price points and then extends into the future to act as a line of support or resistance.

UPTREND LINE

An uptrend line has a positive slope and is formed by connecting two or more **low** points. The second low must be higher than the first for the line to have a positive slope. Note that at least three points must be connected

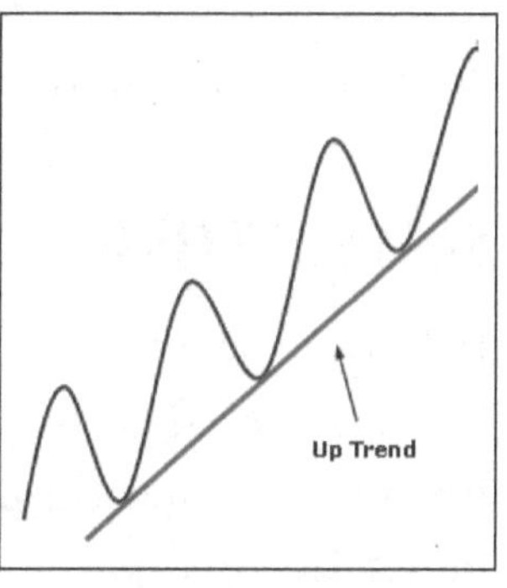

before the line is considered to be a valid Trend line.

Uptrend lines act as support. As long as prices remain above the trend line, the uptrend is considered solid and intact. A break below the uptrend line indicates that net-demand has weakened and a change in trend could be imminent.

DOWNTREND LINE

A downtrend line has a negative slope and is formed by connecting two or more **high** points. The second high must be lower than the first for the line to have a negative slope. Note that at least three points must be connected before the line is considered to be a valid trendline.

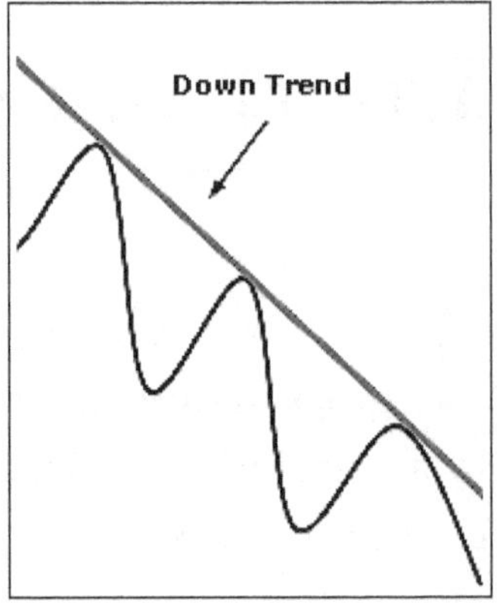

Downtrend lines act as resistance. As long as prices remain below the downtrend line, the downtrend is solid and intact. A break above the downtrend line indicates that net-supply is decreasing and that a change of trend could be imminent.

SCALE SETTINGS

If long-term trend lines are being drawn or when there is a large change in price. It is better to draw the trend line on the logarithmic chart also and check which one is better fitting.

An arithmetic scale displays incremental values (15,20,25,30) evenly as they move up the y-axis while A log scale displays incremental values in percentage terms as they move up the y-axis.

A Rs.10 movement in price will look the same from Rs.10 to Rs.20 or from Rs.100 to Rs.110. A move from Rs.10 to Rs.20 is a 100% gain and would appear to be much larger than a move from Rs.100 to Rs.110, which is only a 10% gain.

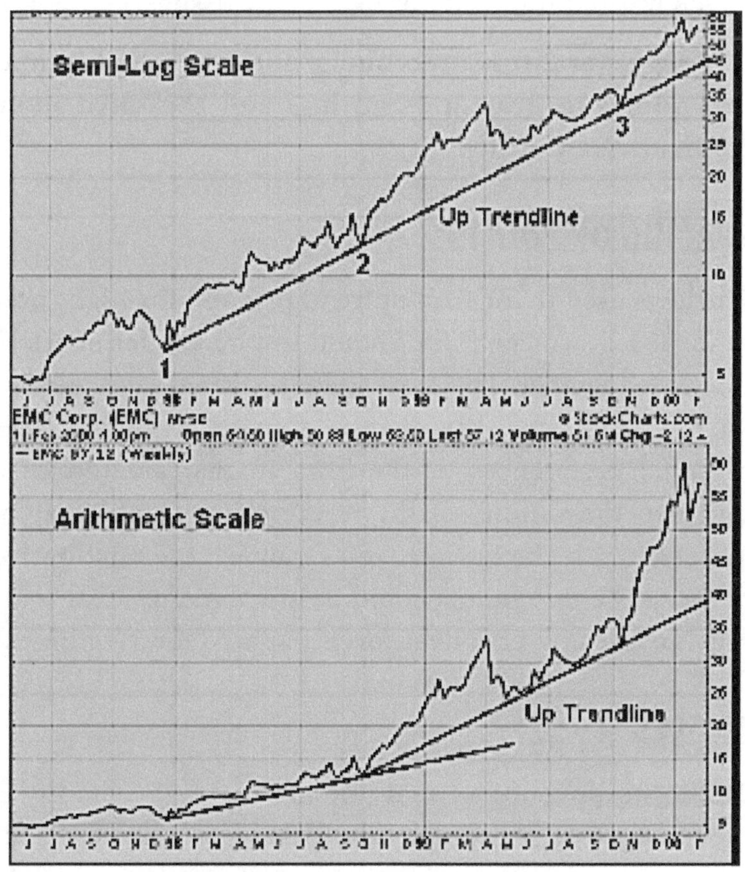

VALIDATION

It takes two or more points to draw a trend line. The more points used to draw the trend line, the more validity attached to the support or resistance level represented by the trend line. It can sometimes be difficult to find more than 2 points from which to construct a trend line. Even though trend lines are an important aspect of technical analysis, it is not always possible to draw trend lines on every price chart. Sometimes the lows or highs just don't match up, and it is best not to force the issue.

The general rule in technical analysis is that it takes two points to draw a trend line and the third point confirms the validity.

SPACING OF POINTS

The lows used to form an uptrend line and the highs used to form a downtrend line should not be too far apart, or too close together. The most suitable distance will depend on the timeframe, the degree of price movement, and personal preferences. If the lows (highs) are too close together, the validity of the reaction low (high) may be in question. If the lows are too far apart, the relationship between the two points could be suspect. An ideal trend line is made up of relatively evenly spaced lows (or highs).

ANGLES

As the steepness of a trend line increases, the validity of the support or resistance level decreases. A steep trend line results from a sharp advance (or decline) over a brief period of time. The angle of a trend line created from such sharp moves is unlikely to offer a meaningful support or resistance level. Even if the trend line is formed with three seemingly valid points, it will be very difficult to use this trend line for getting signal of break out or Support and Resistance.

CONCLUSION

Trend lines can offer great insight, but if used improperly, they can also produce false signals. Other items - such as horizontal support and resistance levels or peak-and-trough analysis - should be employed to validate trend line breaks.

While trend lines have become a very popular aspect of technical analysis, they are merely one tool for establishing, analyzing, and confirming a trend.

By using trend line breaks for warnings, traders can pay closer attention to other confirming signals for a potential change in trend.

~~~
~~~

CHAPTER 17
Support & Resistance

When inexperienced traders and beginners open up their trading platform in the morning, most of them will only see choppy and unconnected price behaviour on the screen. Experienced traders, on the other hand, will immediately try to identify various patterns, trends, swing highs and lows, and potential support & resistance zones.

Unexperienced eyes tend to perceive market behaviour as irrational and messy, but the truth is that most of the price action can be systematised into organised patterns and movements. One of these patterns is Support and resistance.

SUPPORT

A support level is a level where the price tends to find support as it falls. This means that the price is more likely to "bounce" off this level rather than break through it.

However, once the price has breached this level, by an amount exceeding some noise, it is likely to continue falling until meeting another support level.

The support price is a price at which one can expect more buyers than sellers. The support level is always below the current market price. There is a maximum likely hood that the price could fall till the support, consolidate, absorb all the demand, and then start to move upwards. The support is one of the critical technical level market participants look for in a falling market. The support often acts as a trigger to buy.

RESISTANCE

A Resistance level is the opposite of a support level. It is where the price tends to find resistance as it rises. Again, this means that the price is more likely to "bounce" off this level rather than break through it. However, once the price has breached this level, by an amount exceeding some noise, it is likely to continue rising until meeting another resistance level.

Resistance price is a price at which one can expect more sellers than buyers.

The resistance level is always above the current market price. The likely hood of the price rising up to the resistance level, consolidating, absorbing all the supply, and then declining is high. The resistance is one of the critical technical analysis tools which market participants look at in a rising market. The resistance often acts as a trigger to sell.

IDENTIFYING SUPPORT & RESISTANCE LEVELS

Support and resistance levels can be identified by trend lines.

The more often a support/resistance level is "tested" (touched and bounced off by price), the more significance is given to that specific level.

If a price breaks past a support level, that support level often becomes a new resistance level. The opposite is true as well; if price breaks a resistance level, it will often find support at that level in the future.

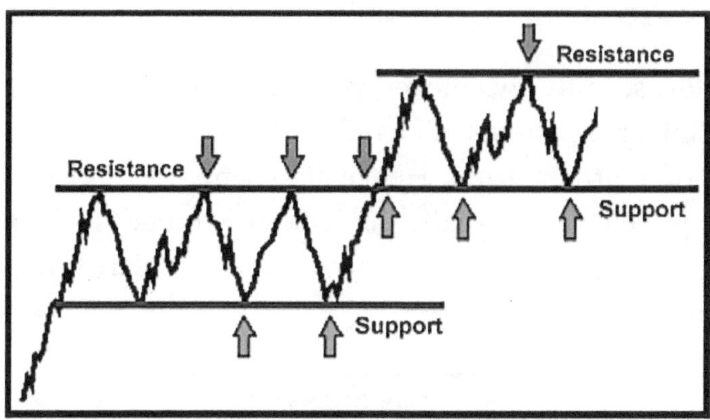

Psychological Support and Resistance levels form an important part of a trader's technical analysis. As price reaches a value ending in 50 or 100 (ex. 250 0r 300), people often see these levels as a strong potential for interruption in the current movement. The price may hit the line and reverse, it could hover around the level as Bulls and Bears fight for supremacy, or it may punch straight through. A trader should always exercise caution when approaching

00 levels in general, and 50 levels if it has previously acted as Support or Resistance.

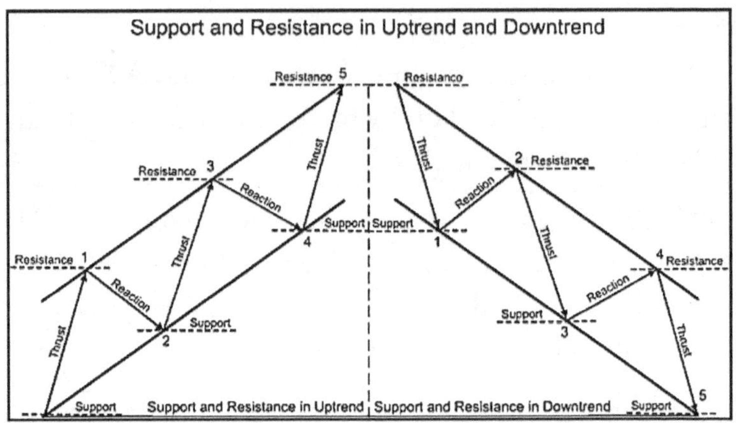

Please note, whenever you run a visual exercise in Technical Analysis such as identifying S&R, you run the risk of approximation. Hence always give room for error. The price level is usually depicted in a range and not at a single price point. It is actually a zone or an area that acts as support or resistance.

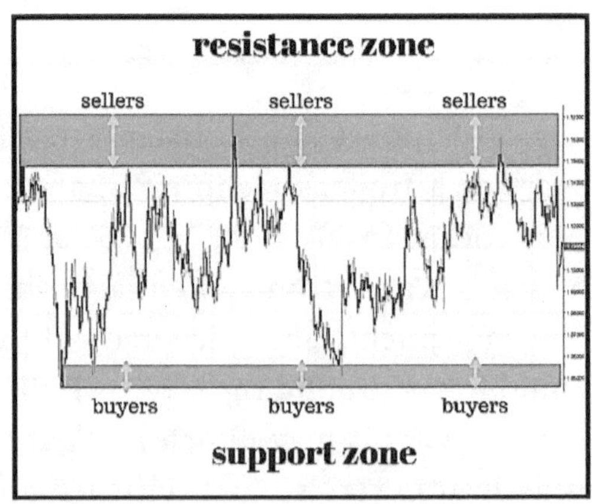

CONCLUSION

The support and resistance lines are only indicative of a possible reversal of prices. They, by no means should be taken for as certain. Like anything else in technical analysis, one should weigh the possibility of an event occurring (based on patterns) in terms of probability.

~~~
~~~

CHAPTER 18
Chart Patterns & Its Significance

In this chapter, we will discuss few chart patterns which are quite famous among traders as success rate of these patterns are quite high.

FLAG & PENNANTS CHART PATTERNS

Flags and pennants can be categorized as continuation patterns. They usually represent only brief pauses in a dynamic market. They are typically seen right after a big, quick move. The market then usually takes off again in the same direction. Research has shown that these patterns are some of the most reliable continuation patterns.

(a) Bullish flags are characterized by lower tops and lower bottoms, with the pattern slanting against the trend and their trendlines run parallel.

(b)   Bearish flags are comprised of higher tops and higher bottoms. "Bear" flags also have a tendency to slope against the trend. Their trendlines run parallel as well.

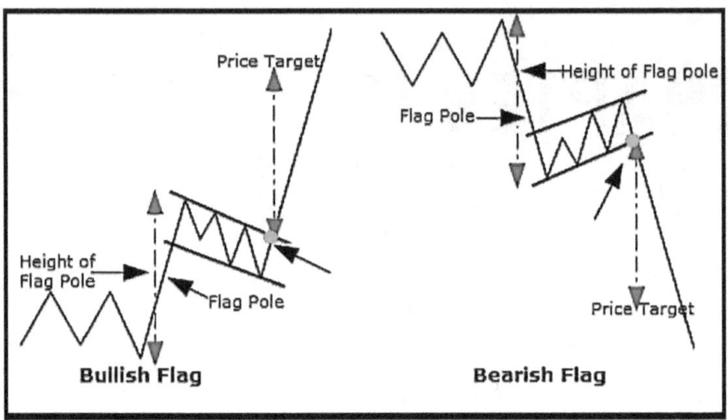

(c)   Bullish Pennants looks very much like symmetrical triangles. These occur after an uptrend.

(d)   Bearish Pennants looks very much like symmetrical triangles. These occur after a downtrend

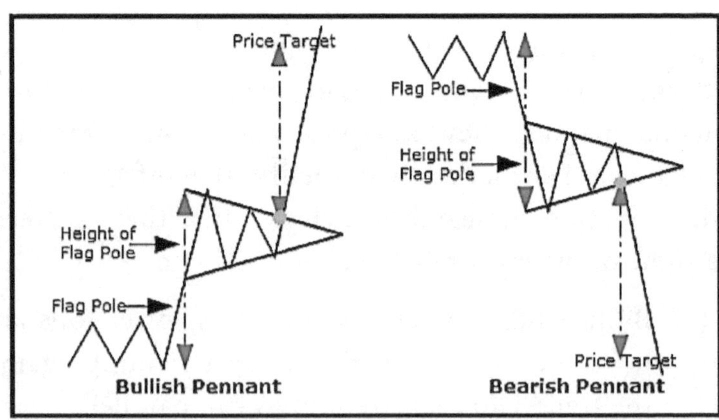

WEDGES

The wedge formation is also similar to a symmetrical triangle in appearance, in that they have converging trendlines that come together at an apex. However, wedges are distinguished by a noticeable slant, either to the upside or to the downside. (As with triangles, volume should diminish during its formation and increase on its resolve.)

Wedges can be divided in two parts

- Falling Wedges
- Rising Wedges

Falling Wedges

A falling wedge is generally considered bullish and is usually found in uptrends. But they can also be found in downtrends as well. The implication, however, is still generally bullish. This pattern is marked by a series of lower tops and lower bottoms.

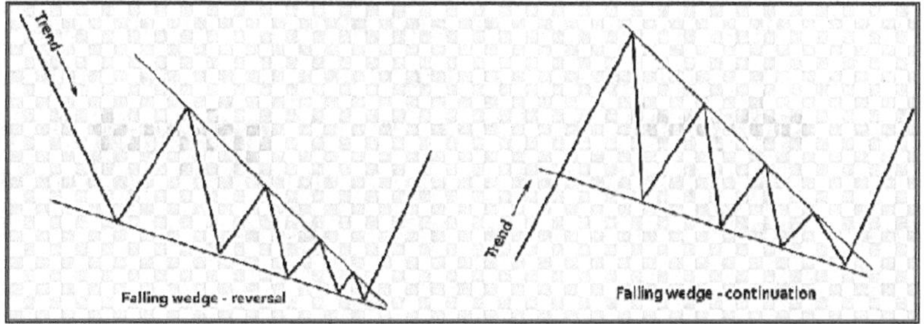

Rising Wedges

A rising wedge is generally considered bearish and is usually found in downtrends. They can be found in uptrends too, but would still generally be regarded as bearish. Rising wedges put in a series of higher tops and higher bottoms.

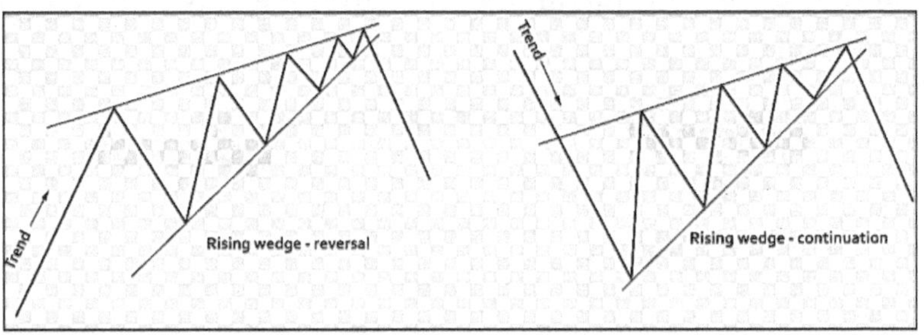

CUP & HANDLE CHART PATTERNS

A cup and handle price pattern on charts is a technical indicator that resembles a cup and handle where the cup is in the shape of a "U" and the handle has a slight downward drift. The right-hand side of the pattern typically has a low trading volume. A cup and handle is considered a bullish continuation pattern and is used to identify buying opportunities. Traders should Enter at Breakout (slightly above the upper trend line of the handle). Stop loss is below handle. Target is the depth of the Cup.

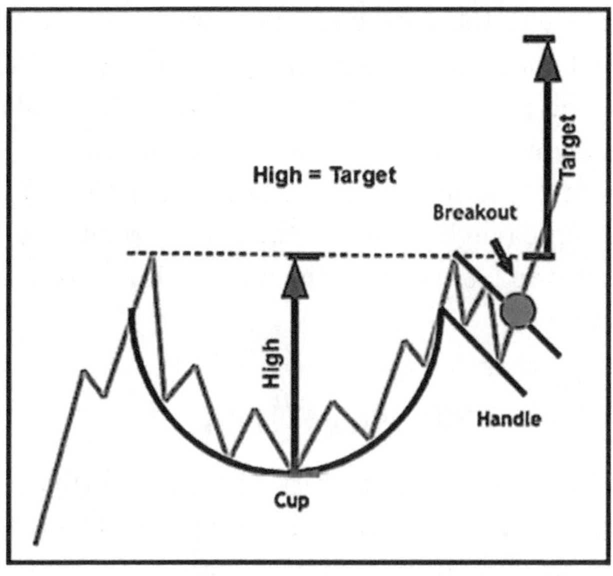

INVERTED CUP & HANDLE CHART PATTERNS

An Inverted cup and handle price pattern on charts is a technical indicator that resembles an Inverted cup and

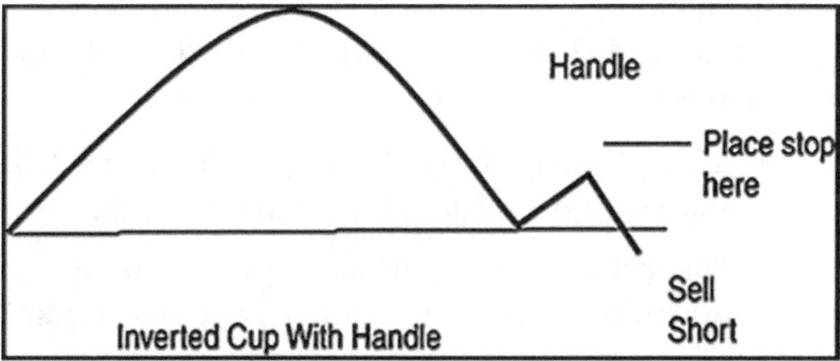

handle where the cup is in the shape of a inverted "U" and the handle has a slight upward drift. The right-hand side of the pattern typically has a low trading volume. It is considered a bearish continuation pattern and is used to identify shorting opportunities. Traders should Enter at Breakout (slightly below the lower trend line of the handle). Stop loss is above the handle. Target is the depth of the Cup.

HEAD AND SHOULDER PATTERN

A head and shoulders pattern is a chart formation that resembles a baseline with three peaks, the outside two are close in height and the middle is highest.

A head and shoulders pattern describes a specific Chart Pattern that predicts a bullish-to-bearish trend reversal.

The head and shoulders pattern is believed to be one of the most reliable trend reversal patterns.

A head and shoulders pattern is comprised of three components:

- After long bullish trends, the price rises to a peak and subsequently declines to form a trough.
- The price rises again to form a second high substantially above the initial peak and declines again.
- The price rises a third time, but only to the level of the first peak, before declining once more.

- The first and third peaks are shoulders, and the second peak forms the head. The line connecting the first and second troughs is called the neckline.

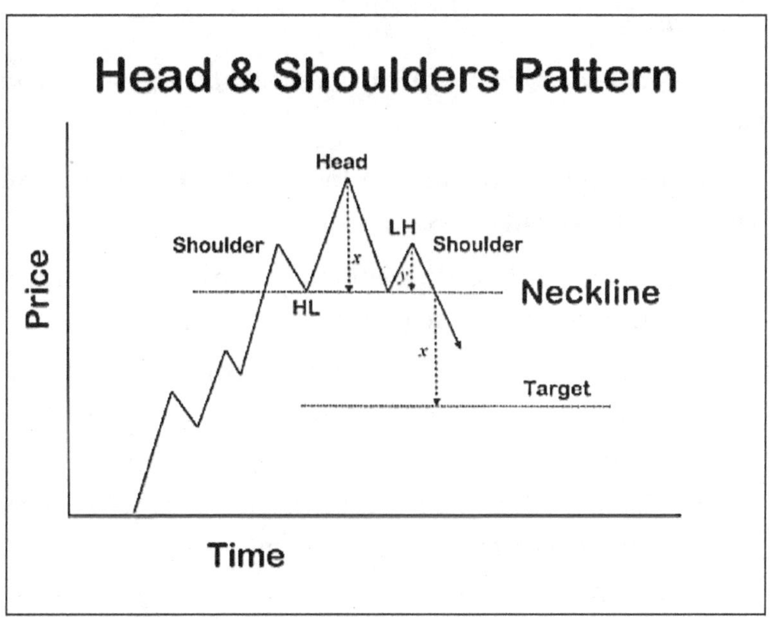

Entry

When price breaks the neckline

Target

Height of Head from neckline

Stop Loss

Just above Shoulder

Inverted Head and Shoulders

An Inverted head and shoulders pattern describe a specific Chart Pattern that predicts a bearish-to-bullish trend reversal.

It is believed to be one of the most reliable trend reversal patterns.

An Inverted head and shoulders pattern is comprised of three component parts:

- After a long bearish trend, the price declines to form a trough and subsequently rises to form a peak.

- The price decline again to form a second low substantially below the initial trough and rises again.

- The price declines a third time, but only to the level of the first trough, before rising once more

- The first and third peaks are shoulders, and the second peak forms the head. The line connecting the first and second troughs is called the neckline.

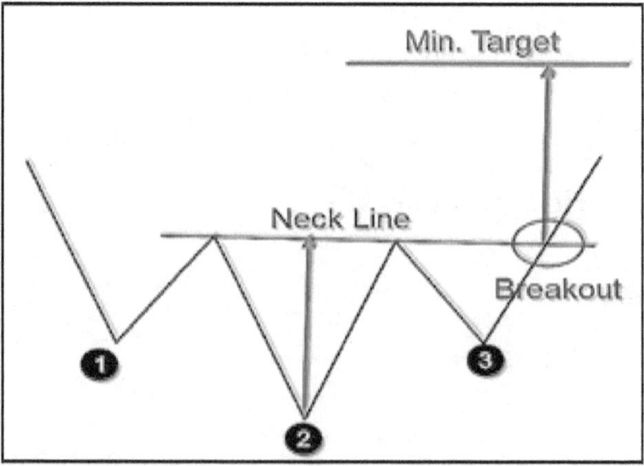

Once the final trough is made, the price heads upward, toward the resistance found near the top of the previous troughs.

Entry

When price breaks the neckline

Target

Depth of the Inverted Head from neckline

Stop Loss

Just below the Inverted Shoulder

GAPS

A gap is a change in price levels between the close and open of two consecutive time frame of same duration.

Gaps are areas on a chart where the price of a stock moves sharply up or down, with no trading in between. As a result, you can observe it in the stock's chart.

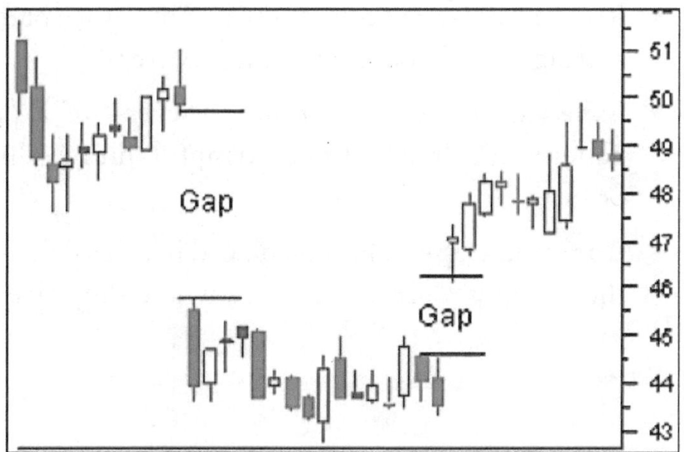

Typically, Gaps are of two types namely Full Gap & Partial Gap:

- **Gap-up:** When the price of a financial instrument opens higher than the previous day's price, it is gap-up.

- **Gap-down:** When the price of a financial instrument opens lower than the previous trading day it is gap-down. Gap-downs occur when there is a change in investor sentiments.

- **Partial gap-up:** A partial gap-up in the stock market occurs when there is a rise in the opening prices but the price is not higher than the previous day's high price.

- **Partial gap-down:** A partial gap down in stock market occurs when the opening price is below the previous closing price, but not below previous day's low.

Gaps can be classified into four groups:

- **Breakaway Gaps** occur at the end of a price pattern and signal the beginning of a new trend.

- **Exhaustion Gaps** occur near the end of a price pattern and signal a final attempt to hit new highs or lows.

- **Common Gaps** cannot be placed in a price pattern, they simply represent an area where the price has gapped.

- **Continuation gaps** occur in the middle of a price pattern and signal a rush of buyers or sellers who share a common belief in the underlying stock's future direction.

Meaning of Gap Filled or Not Filled

When someone says a gap has been filled, that means the price has moved back to the original pre-gap level. These fills are quite common and occur because of the following:

- **Irrational behaviour of Retail trader:** The initial spike may have been overly optimistic or pessimistic, therefore inviting a correction.

- **Technical resistance**: When a price moves up or down sharply, it doesn't leave behind any support or resistance

- **Price Pattern**: Price patterns are used to classify gaps and can tell you if a gap will be filled or not. Exhaustion gaps are typically the most likely to be filled because they signal the end of a price trend, while continuation and breakaway Gaps are significantly less likely to be filled since they are used to confirm the direction of the current trend.

How to Play the Gaps

There are many ways to take advantage of these gaps, but I will suggest you following as it has more chances of success and risk will be less.

- Once a stock has started to fill the gap, it will rarely stop, because there is often no immediate support or resistance.

- Exhaustion gaps and continuation gaps predict the price moving in two different directions – be sure you correctly classify the gap you are going to play.

- Retail traders are the ones who usually exhibit irrational exuberance; however, smart money may play along to help their portfolios, so be careful when using this indicator and wait for the price to start to break before taking a position.

- Be sure to watch the volume. High Volume should be present in breakaway gaps while low volume should occur in exhaustion gaps.

~~~
~~~

CHAPTER 19
Moving Average

All of us have learnt about averages in school, moving average is just an extension of that. Moving averages are trend indicators and are frequently used due to their simplicity and effectiveness. Before we learn moving averages, let us have a quick recap on how averages are calculated.

Assume, Runs scored by 10 players in a match are as per following.

78, 85, 85, 54, 64, 50, 95, 35, 60, 79

Average = Total Runs/no. of players

= (78+85+85+54+64+50+95+35+60+79) / 10

= 685/10

= 68.5

From above, we can understand the average in a way that if every player had scored 68.5 runs, total runs of the team would be 685.

Now we will understand how to calculate the moving average.

Let us take an example of Yes Bank:

Moving Average Calculation for YES BANK

Row Ref Name	Date	Close Price	5 day Moving avg	Average Formula
A	14-01-2019	195.40		
B	15-01-2019	202.95		
C	16-01-2019	208.35		
D	17-01-2019	201.45		
E	18-01-2019	198.25		
F	21-01-2019	192.10	201.28	(A+B+C+D+E)/5
G	22-01-2019	192.10	200.62	(B+C+D+E+F)/5
H	23-01-2019	197.30	198.45	(C+D+E+F+G)/5
I	24-01-2019	213.85	196.24	(D+E+F+G+H)/5
J	25-01-2019	219.65	198.72	(E+F+G+H+I)/5
K	28-01-2019	207.65	203.00	(F+G+H+I+J)/5
L	29-01-2019	202.60	206.11	(G+H+I+J+K)/5
M	30-01-2019	199.40	208.21	(H+I+J+K+L)/5
N	31-01-2019	194.30	208.63	(I+J+K+L+M)/5
O	01-02-2019	185.65	204.72	(J+K+L+M+N)/5
P	04-02-2019	179.90	197.92	(K+L+M+N+O)/5
Q	05-02-2019	175.80	192.37	(L+M+N+O+P)/5
R	06-02-2019	176.30	187.01	(M+N+O+P+Q)/5
S	07-02-2019	176.75	182.39	(N+O+P+Q+R)/5
T	08-02-2019	174.80	178.88	(O+P+Q+R+S)/5

For calculating 5 day Moving average, we will start from 21.01.2019 i.e. row F, as we need a minimum 5 day data.

Previous 5 day closing average of row F will be

= (closing price of 14th Jan + closing price of 15th Jan + closing price of 16th Jan + closing price of 17th Jan + closing price of 18th Jan) / 5

= (195.4+202.95+208.35+201.45+198.25)/5

= 1006.4/5

= 201.28

Similarly, we will calculate the previous 5 day average for 22.01.2019 as per following

= (closing price of 15th Jan + closing price of 16th Jan + closing price of 17th Jan + closing price of 18th Jan+ closing price of 21st Jan) / 5

= (202.95+208.35+201.45+198.25+192.10)/5

= 1003.1/5

= 200.62

Similarly, the average of the last 5 days is calculated for balance dates.

So essentially, we are moving to the latest data point and discarding the oldest to calculate the latest 5 day average. Hence the name "moving" average!

A moving average as calculated above is called a 'Simple Moving Average' (SMA).

Since we are calculating it as per the latest 5 days of data it is called 5 Day SMA. Similarly, we can obtain

5 min, 15 min, 1 hour, 10 day, 20 day, 50 day, 200 day SMA for any script.

Any time frame can be selected from the charting software based on your requirements.

The averages for the 5 day are then joined to form a smooth curving line known as the moving average line, and it continues to move as the time progresses.

EXPONENTIAL MOVING AVERAGE (EMA)

Refer the same table of YES Bank which we used for explaining Simple Moving average. Here we have given equal weightage to each data point to calculate the Simple moving average. Meaning, we are assuming that the data point on 14th Jan is as important as the data point on 18th Jan. However, when it comes to markets, this may not be always true

Remember the basic assumption of technical analysis – markets discount everything. This means the latest price that you see (on 18th Jan) discounts all the known and unknown information. This also implies the price on 18th is more sacred than the price on 14th.

Using this logic, we would like to assign weightage to data points based on the 'newness' of the data. Therefore, the data point on 18th Jan gets the highest weightage, 17th Jan gets the next highest weightage, 16th Jan gets the 3rd highest, and so on.

By doing so, we have scaled the data points according to its newness – the latest data point gets the maximum weightage and the oldest data point gets the least weightage.

The average calculated on this scaled set of numbers gives us the Exponential Moving Average (EMA). We will be skipping the EMA calculation part, simply because most of the technical analysis software lets us drag and drop the EMA on prices. Hence we will focus on EMA's application instead of its calculation.

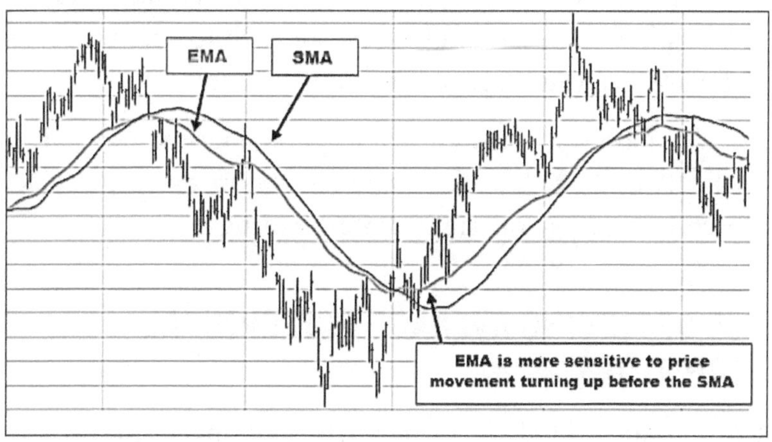

COMPARISON OF SMA VS EMA

The SMA and EMA are calculated differently and it is the calculation that makes the EMA quicker to react to price changes and the SMA react slower. That is the main difference between the two.

Sometimes the EMA will react quickly, causing a trader to get out of a trade on a market hiccup while the slower-moving SMA keeps the person in the trade, resulting in a bigger profit after the hiccup is finished. At other times, the opposite could happen. The faster moving EMA signals trouble quicker than the SMA, and so the EMA trader gets out of harm's way quicker, saving that person time and money.

Each trader must decide which MA is better for his particular strategy. Many shorter-term traders use EMAs because they want to be alerted as soon as the price is moving the other way. Longer-term traders tend to rely on SMAs since these investors aren't in rush to act and prefer to be less actively engaged in their trades.

Ultimately, it comes down to personal preference. Plot an EMA and SMA of the same length on a chart and see which one helps you make better trading decisions.

USE OF MOVING AVERAGE IN TECHNICAL INDICATORS

Combination of short term SMA Vs Long term SMA or same term SMA Vs EMA is used to predict the direction of the trend. We will explore it in detail in subsequent chapters.

~~~
~~~

CHAPTER 20
Volume

Understanding the effect of Volumes is very important in Technical Analysis. We can visualise a lot about the price movement after having a look on the traded Volumes of a stock.

Volumes indicate how many shares are bought and sold over a given period of time. Suppose, you purchased 100 shares of Tata motors and of course, somebody sold you 100 shares of Tata Motors, then total volume traded will be 100. (Do not take it as 200).

UNDERSTANDING VOLUME TREND

Volume information of any stock is of no use as we can not deduce anything if Stock A is having the double volume that the Stock B. The only information we can get that Stock A is more liquid than Stock B. e.g. volumes of YES Bank on 14th Feb was 75,34,839. So how useful is this information when reading in isolation? If you think about it, it has no merit and hence would actually mean nothing. However, when you associate today's volume information with the preceding price and volume trend, then volume information becomes a lot more meaningful.

In the table below you will find a summary of how to use volume information:

Row no.	Price	Volume	Expectation
1	Increasing	Increasing	Bullish
2	Increasing	Decreasing	Price reversal may happen as smart money is not involved in this Price increase
3	Decreasing	Increasing	Bearish
4	Decreasing	Decreasing	Price reversal may happen as smart money is not involved in this Price decrease

Now let us understand what does increase in Volume means? What is the reference point? Should it be an increase over the previous day's volume or the previous week's cumulative volume?

As a practice, traders usually compare today's volume over the average of the last 22 days volume. Generally, the rule of thumb is as follows:

High Volume: Today's volume > last 22 days average volume

Low Volume: Today's volume < last 22 days average volume

Average Volume: Today's volume is around the last 22 days average volume

To get this information, you have to draw a 22days SMA & 3 days SMA on the volume bars. **When 3 day SMA crosses 22 day SMA from below to above, it signifies Volume is increasing & when 3 day SMA crosses 22 day SMA from above to below, it signifies Volume is decreasing.**

How to interpret the relation between Price and Volume

When institutional investors buy or sell they obviously do not transact in small volume e.g. LIC of India who is one of the biggest domestic institutional investors in India. If they would buy Sunpharma, would you think they would buy 500 shares? Obviously not, they would probably buy 400,000 shares or even more. Now, if they were to buy 400,000 shares from the open market, it will start reflecting in volumes. Besides, because they are buying a large chunk of shares, the share price also tends to go up.

Usually, institutional money is referred to as "smart money". It is perceived that 'smart money' always makes wiser moves in the market compared to retail traders. Hence following the smart money seems like a good idea.

Row 1: Price increasing & Volume increasing

If both the price and the volume are increasing as shown in Row 1, It only signifies that smart Money is showing interest in the stock. Going by the assumption that smart money always makes smart choices the expectation turns bullish and hence one should look at buying opportunity in the stock.

It also implies that whenever you decide to buy, ensure that the volumes are substantial. This means that you are buying along with the smart money.

Row 2: Price increasing & Volume decreasing

Now let us understand 2nd row. What if the price is increasing but Volume is decreasing.

As Price is increasing, it simply means that someone is buying but Smart money is not involved as Volume is decreasing. Now, who is this Some One? Most probably it is the small retail participation.

As Smart Money is not participating, You need to be extra cautious as it may be a possible bull trap and Price could soon reverse.

Row 3: Price decreasing, Volume Increasing

If Price is decreasing, but Volume is increasing, It means that smart money is selling. It also means that smart money has some information which is still not in public domain. Going by assumption that smart money always makes smart choices, you should think to come out from your stock holding, if any. You can also look for any shorting opportunity here.

Row 4: Price decreasing & Volume decreasing

Decreasing Volume simply means that Smart money is not selling. But Price is decreasing, it means that sellers are more than buyers. If we combine both of these information, it signifies danger of being trapped as Price could reverse soon if suddenly smart money decides to buy the stock.

~~~
~~~

CHAPTER 21
Technical Indicators

Trading without indicators is like running blindfold and it encourages emotional trading. You trade with hope and ultimately hope become fear. Use of indicators makes life easier for traders to take a more objective decision.

Indicators serve three broad functions: **To alert, To confirm and To predict**.

- An indicator can act as an **alert** to study price action a little more closely. If momentum is waning, it may be a signal to watch for a break of support. Or, if there is a large positive divergence building, it may serve as an alert to watch for a resistance breakout.

- Indicators can be used to **confirm** other technical analysis tools. If there is a breakout on the price chart, a corresponding moving average crossover could serve to confirm the breakout.

- Some investors and traders use indicators to predict the direction of future prices.

Indicators are built on a pre-set logic using which traders can supplement their technical study (candlesticks, volumes, Support & Resistance) to arrive at a trading decision. Indicators help in buying, selling, confirming trends, and sometimes predicting trends.

There are more than a ton of technical indicators available and also being made every week, but here, we will study few indicators and understand the logic behind these. Our purpose is not to get a doctorate degree in Indicators but to become Money Maker.

Indicators can be divided into two types. Leading Indicator & lagging indicator.

Leading indicator

As the name suggest this type of indicators leads the price and usually signals the occurrence of a reversal or a new trend in advance but these are notorious for giving false signals. Therefore, you should be highly alert while using leading indicators, but with experience, you will increase the efficiency of leading indicators.

A majority of leading indicators are called oscillators as they oscillate within a bounded range. Generally, an oscillator oscillates between two extreme values e.g. 0 to 100. Based on the oscillator's reading (for example 25, 80 etc) the trading interpretation varies.

Lagging indicator

As the name suggests, these indicators lag the price; meaning it usually signals the occurrence of a reversal or a new trend after it has occurred. You may think, what would be the use of getting a signal after the event has occurred? Remember, In technical analysis, we never try to pick up the exact bottom or Top of a trend.

TECHNICAL INDICATORS

Indicators can also be sub-divided into many categories.

(a) Trend Indicators

Trend trading strategies assume that a security will continue to move along its current trend and often contain a take-profit or stop-loss provision if there are any signs of a reversal. It can be used by short-term, intermediate-term or long-term traders. Regardless of their chosen time frame, traders will remain in their position until they believe the trend has reversed, although reversals may occur at different times for each time frame. Following indicators are used by Trend Traders.

Moving Average – Lagging Indicator (We have already discussed it in Chapter 19)

MACD – Lagging Indicator

ADX – Leading Indicator

(b) Momentum Indicators

Momentum is the measurement of the speed or velocity of price change (price rise as well as price fall). From the standpoint of trending, momentum is a very useful indicator of strength or weakness in the stocks price. Following indicators are used by Momentum Traders.

RSI – Leading Indicator

Stochastic – Leading Indicator

(c) Volatility Indicators

Volatility-based indicators are valuable technical analysis tools that look at changes in market prices over a specified period of time. The faster prices change, the higher the volatility. The slower prices change, the lower the volatility. It can be measured and calculated based on historical prices and can be used for trend identification. Following indicators are used by Traders to ascertain Volatility.

Bollinger Bands   – Lagging Indicator

Average True Range – Lagging Indicator

(d) Volume Indicators

Volume Profile: We have already discussed the basics of a Volume as Indicator in Chapter 20.

~~~
~~~

CHAPTER 22
MACD (Moving Average Convergence/Divergence)

MACD is one of the simplest and most effective momentum indicators available. The MACD turns two trend-following indicators, Moving Average into a momentum oscillator by subtracting the longer moving average from the shorter moving average.

As a result, the MACD offers the best of both worlds: **trend following and momentum.** The MACD fluctuates above and below the zero line as the moving averages converge, cross and diverge. You can look for signal line crossovers, Centerline crossovers and divergences to generate signals

$$MACD = 12 \text{ period EMA} - 26 \text{ period EMA}$$

WHAT DOES MACD TELL YOU?

The MACD has a positive value whenever the 12-period EMA (line touching the candlesticks) is above the 26-period EMA (line far from candle sticks) and a negative value when the 12-period EMA is below the 26-period EMA. The more distant the MACD is above or below its baseline indicates that the distance between the two EMAs is growing. In the following chart, you can see how the two EMAs applied to the price chart correspond to the MACD (black) crossing above or below its baseline (dashed) in the indicator below the price chart.

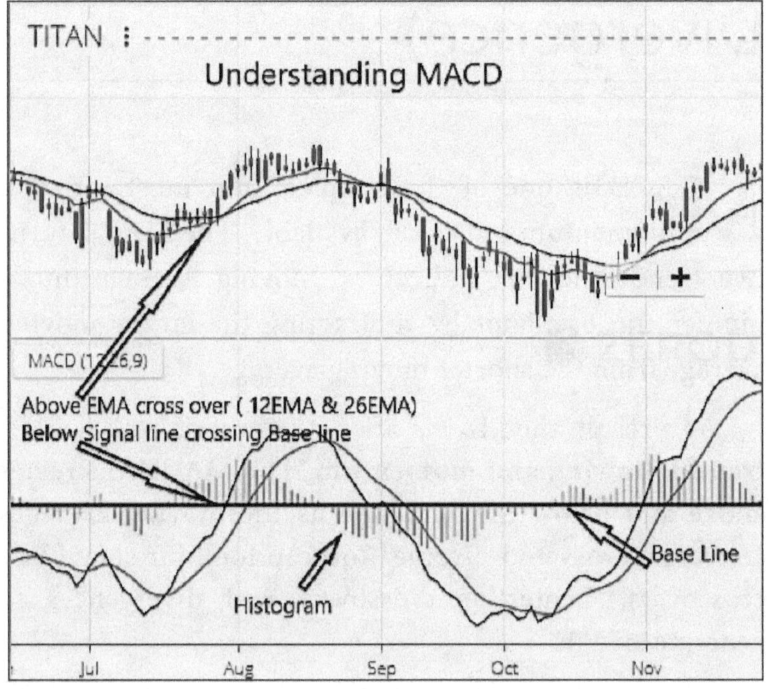

MACD is often displayed with a histogram (see the chart above) which graphs the distance between the MACD and its signal line. If the MACD is above the signal line, the histogram will be above the MACD's baseline. If the MACD is below its signal line, the histogram will be below the MACD's baseline. Traders use the MACD's histogram to identify when bullish or bearish momentum is high.

SIGNAL LINE CROSSOVERS

Signal line crossovers are the most common MACD signals. The signal line is a 9-day EMA of the MACD Line. As a moving average of the indicator, it trails the MACD and makes it easier to spot MACD turns. A bullish crossover occurs when the MACD turns up and crosses above the signal line. A bearish crossover occurs when the MACD turns down and crosses below the signal line. Crossovers can last a few days or a few weeks, it all depends on the strength of the move.

Due diligence is required before relying on these common signals. Signal line crossovers at positive or negative extremes should be viewed with caution. Even though the MACD does not have upper and lower limits, traders can estimate historical extremes with a simple visual assessment. It takes a strong move in the underlying security to push momentum to an extreme. Even though the move may continue, momentum is likely to slow and this will usually produce a signal line crossover at the extremities. Volatility in the underlying security can also increase the number of crossovers.

The chart above shows TITAN with its 12-day EMA, 26-day EMA and the 12,26,9 MACD in the indicator window. There were three signal line crossovers in six months: two up and one down.

CENTERLINE CROSSOVERS

Centerline crossovers are the next most common MACD signals. A bullish centerline crossover occurs when the MACD Line moves above the zero line to turn positive. This happens when the 12-day EMA of the underlying security moves above the 26-day EMA. A bearish centerline crossover occurs when the MACD moves below the zero line to turn negative. This happens when the 12-day EMA moves below the 26-day EMA.

Centerline crossovers can last a few days or a few months. It all depends on the strength of the trend. The MACD will remain positive as long as there is a sustained uptrend. The MACD will remain negative when there is a sustained downtrend.

~~~
~~~

CHAPTER 23
Average Directional Index (ADX)

The Average Directional Index (ADX), Minus Directional Indicator (-DI) and Plus Directional Indicator (+DI) represent a group of directional movement indicators that form a trading system developed by Welles Wilder. Although Wilder designed his Directional Movement System with commodities and it's daily prices in mind, these indicators can also be applied to stocks.

Positive and negative directional movement form the backbone of the Directional Movement System. Wilder determined directional movement by comparing the difference between two consecutive lows with the difference between their respective highs.

The **Plus Directional Indicator (+DI)** and **Minus Directional Indicator (-DI)** measure trend *direction* over time. These two indicators are often referred to collectively as the Directional Movement Indicator (DMI).

The **Average Directional Index (ADX)** is smoothed averages of the difference between +DI and -DI, and measures the *strength* of the trend (regardless of direction) over time.

Using these three indicators together, traders can determine both the **Direction** and **Strength** of the trend.

APPLICATION OF ADX

Calculation part of ADX, (+DI) & (-DI) is a bit complex, so we will not go into it, However, we will learn more about its application.

At its most basic, the Average Directional Index (ADX) can be used to determine if a security is trending or not. This determination helps traders choose between a trend-following system or a non-trend-following system. Wilder suggests that a strong trend is present when ADX is above 25 and no trend is present when below 20. There appears to be a gray zone between 20 and 25. As noted above, traders may need to adjust the settings to increase sensitivity and signals. ADX also has a fair amount of lag because of all the smoothing techniques. Many technical analysts use 20 as the key level for ADX.

The Average Directional Index (ADX) is used to measure the strength or weakness of a trend, not the actual direction. Directional movement is defined by +DI and -DI. In general, the bulls have the edge when +DI is greater than -DI, while the bears have the edge when -DI is greater than +DI. Crosses of these directional indicators can be combined with ADX for a complete trading system.

Wilder put forth a simple system for trading with these directional movement indicators. The first requirement is "ADX to be trading above 25". This ensures that prices are trending. Many traders, however, use 20 as the key level.

A buy signal occurs when +DI crosses above -DI. Wilder based the initial stop on the low of the signal day. The signal remains in force as long as this low holds, even if +DI crosses back below -DI. Wait for this low to be penetrated before abandoning the signal. This bullish signal is reinforced if/when ADX turns up and the trend strengthens. Once the trend develops and becomes profitable, traders will have to incorporate a stop-loss and trail their stop loss with the trend.

A sell signal triggers when -DI crosses above +DI. The high on the day of the sell signal becomes the initial stop-loss.

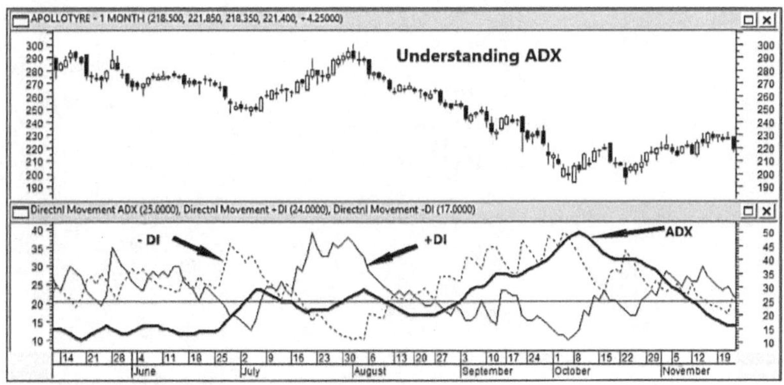

CONCLUSION

The Directional Movement System indicator calculations are complex, interpretation is straightforward, and successful implementation takes practice. +DI and -DI crossovers are quite frequent and you need to filter these signals with complementary analysis. Therefore, you need to look elsewhere for confirmation help. Volume-based indicators, basic trend analysis, and chart patterns can help distinguish strong crossover signals from weak crossover signals.

For example, you can focus on +DI buy signals when the bigger trend is up and -DI sell signals when the bigger trend is down.

~~~
~~~

CHAPTER 24
Momentum Indicators

A t its most fundamental level, momentum is a means of assessing the relative levels of greed and fear in the market at any given point of time. Stocks rise & fall or stuck in a range and such action is measured by oscillators which are powerful leading indicators of the security's immediate direction and its speed.

Price reversal to the downside happens when the power of Bulls is shifted to Bears and generally it does not happen in a whisker. It happens slowly. Though the price is still going up, Bulls are losing their power slowly and Bears are slowly gaining control.

Similarly, Price reversal to the upside happens when the power of Bears is shifted to Bulls and it happens slowly. Though the price is still going down, Bears are losing their power slowly and Bulls are slowly gaining control.

There are few indicators which intimate this change of power beforehand.

We will understand Relative Strength Indicator (RSI) & Stochastics Indicator here.

~~~
~~~

CHAPTER 25
Relative Strength Index (RSI)

Developed by J. Welles Wilder, the Relative Strength Index (RSI) is a momentum oscillator that measures the speed and change of price movements. RSI oscillates between 0 and 100. RSI is considered overbought when above 70 and oversold when below 30. For more conservative view, you can take above 80 as Overbought below 20 as oversold.

Signals can also be generated by looking for divergences, failure swings, and centerline crossovers.

The default look-back period for RSI is 14, but this can be lowered to increase sensitivity or raised to decrease sensitivity. 10-day RSI is more likely to reach overbought or oversold levels than 20-day RSI. The look-back parameters also depend on a security's volatility.

Short-term traders sometimes use 2-period RSI to look for overbought readings above 80 and oversold readings below 20.

DIVERGENCES

According to Wilder, divergences signal a potential reversal point because directional momentum does not confirm the price. A bullish divergence occurs when the underlying security makes a lower low and RSI forms a higher low. RSI does not confirm the lower low and this shows weakening momentum. A bearish divergence forms when the security records a higher high and RSI forms a lower high. RSI does not confirm the new high and this shows weakening momentum.

Refer below Chart of Nifty Future with a bearish divergence in August-September'18. Nifty moved to new highs in August 3rd Week, but RSI formed lower highs for the bearish divergence. The subsequent breakdown in Aug 4th week confirmed weakening momentum.

A bullish divergence formed in Oct 1st week & Oct last week'18. The bullish divergence formed with Nifty moving to new lows in Oct 1st week and RSI holding above its prior low. RSI reflected less downside momentum during the Oct decline. The Nov 1st week breakout confirmed improving upside momentum. Divergences tend to be more robust when they form after an overbought or oversold reading.

Before getting too excited about divergences as great trading signals, it must be noted that divergences are misleading in a strong trend. A strong uptrend can show numerous bearish divergences before a top actually materializes.

Points to note down

- RSI tends to fluctuate between 40 and 90 in a strong bull market (uptrend) with the 40-50 zones acting as support.

- RSI tends to fluctuate between 10 and 60 in a strong bear market (downtrend) with the 50-60 zone acting as resistance.

CONCLUSION

RSI is a versatile momentum oscillator that has stood the test of time. Despite changes in Volatility and the markets over the years, RSI remains as relevant now as it was in Wilder's days. Wilder considers overbought conditions ripe for a reversal, but overbought can also be a sign of strength.

~~~
~~~

CHAPTER 26
Stochastic Oscillator

Developed by George C. Lane in the late 1950s, the Stochastic Oscillator is a momentum indicator that shows the location of the close relative to the high-low range over a set number of periods. According to an interview with Lane, the Stochastic Oscillator "doesn't follow price, it doesn't follow volume or anything like that. It follows the speed or the momentum of price.

As a rule, the momentum changes direction before price." As such, bullish and bearish divergences in the Stochastic Oscillator can be used to forecast reversals. It is also used to identify bull and bear set-ups to anticipate a future reversal. As Stochastic Oscillator is range bound, is also useful for identifying overbought and oversold levels.

CALCULATION

%K = (Current Close – Lowest Low)/(Highest High-Lowest Low)*100

%D = 3 day SMA of %K.

The default setting for the Stochastic Oscillator is 14 periods, which can be days, weeks, months or an intraday timeframe. A 14-period %K would use the most recent close, the highest high over the last 14 periods and the lowest low over the last 14 periods. %D is a 3-day simple moving average of %K. This line is plotted alongside %K to act as a signal or trigger line.

In a simple language, suppose a stock is trading between 100 & 120 in the last 14 days and if current close is at 116. The stochastic will be

= (116-100)/(120-100)*100

= 80%

Fast Stochastic Oscillator:

- Fast %K = %K basic calculation
- Fast %D = 3-period SMA of Fast %K

Slow Stochastic Oscillator:

- Slow %K = Fast %K smoothed with 3-period SMA
- Slow %D = 3-period SMA of Slow %K

The Full Stochastic Oscillator is a fully customizable version of the Slow Stochastic Oscillator. Users can set the look-back period, the number of periods to slow %K and the number of periods for the %D moving average.

Full Stochastic Oscillator:

- Full %K = Fast %K smoothed with X-period SMA
- Full %D = X-period SMA of Full %K

OVERBOUGHT OVERSOLD

As a bound oscillator, the Stochastic Oscillator makes it easy to identify overbought and oversold levels. The oscillator ranges from 0 to 100. No matter how fast a security advances or declines, the Stochastic Oscillator will always fluctuate within this range. Traditional settings use 80 as the overbought threshold and 20 as the oversold threshold. These levels can be adjusted to suit analytical needs and security characteristics

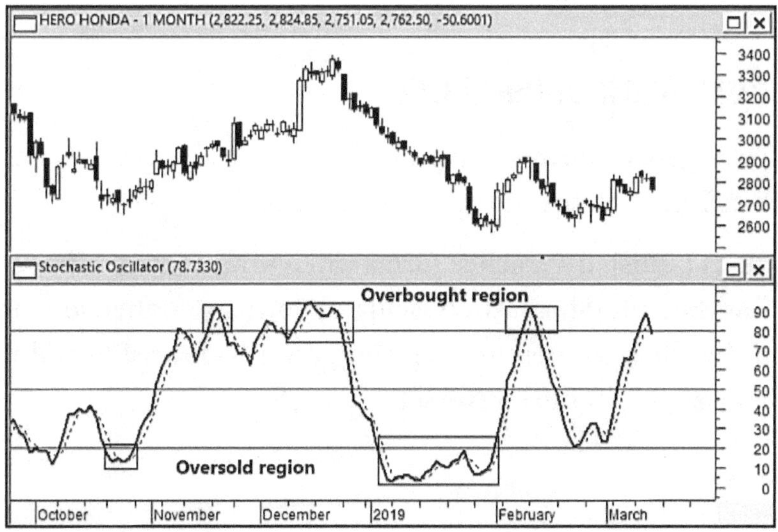

Please make a point that overbought readings are not always bearish. Securities can become overbought and remain overbought during a strong uptrend. Closing levels that are consistently near the top of the range indicate continuous buying pressure.

Similarly, oversold readings are not necessarily bullish. Securities can also become oversold and remain oversold during a strong downtrend. Closing levels consistently near the bottom of the range indicate sustained selling pressure.

It is, therefore, important to identify the bigger trend and trade in the direction of this trend. Look for occasional oversold readings in an uptrend and ignore frequent overbought readings. Similarly, look for occasional overbought readings in a strong downtrend and ignore frequent oversold readings.

BULL BEAR DIVERGENCES

Divergences form when a new high or low in price is not confirmed by the Stochastic Oscillator.

A bullish divergence forms when price records a lower low, but the Stochastic Oscillator forms a higher low. It shows that momentum is losing towards downside and it may signify Bullish reversal.

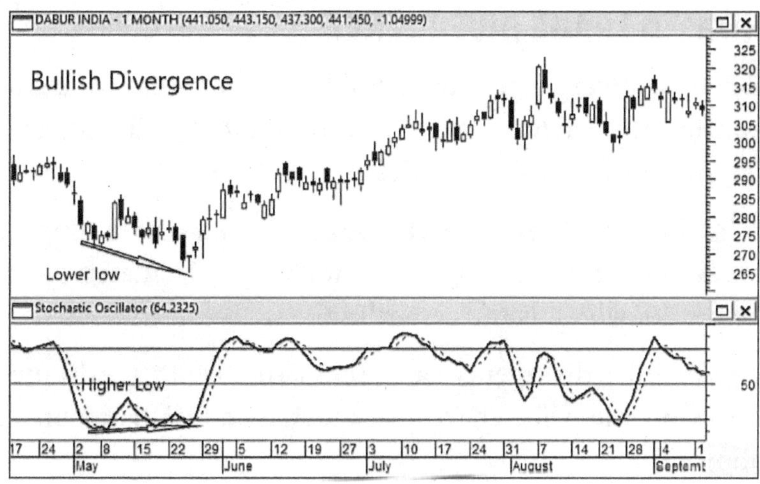

A bearish divergence forms when price records a higher high, but the Stochastic Oscillator forms a lower high. It shows that momentum is losing towards upside and it may signify a bearish reversal.

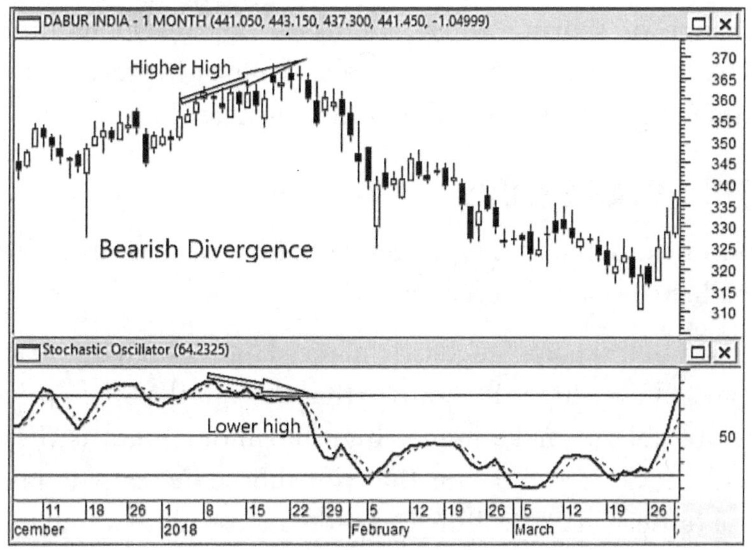

HOW TO TRADE DIVERGENCE

Once a divergence takes hold, You should look for confirmation from other indicators such as Resistance/ Support break or Candlestick reversals.

A bearish divergence can be confirmed with a support break on the price chart or a Stochastic Oscillator break below 50, which is the centerline.

A bullish divergence can be confirmed with a resistance break on the price chart or a Stochastic Oscillator break above 50.

50 is an important level to watch as Stochastic Oscillator moves between zero and one hundred, which makes 50 the centerline.

Just think of it as the 50-meters line in a 100 meter Hockey play ground. The attacking team has a higher chance of scoring when it crosses the 50- meter line. The defence team has an edge as long as it prevents the attacking team from crossing the 50-meter line.

BULL BEAR SETUPS

Bull Bear Setups are type of divergence only but inverse of Bullish/Bearish divergence.

In bull set-up, Stochastic makes Higher high but Price makes lower high. It signifies that though the Stock price is not able to make higher high but momentum is there with stock. It also means that you should be ready to take the trade as next decline is expected to result in a tradable bottom.

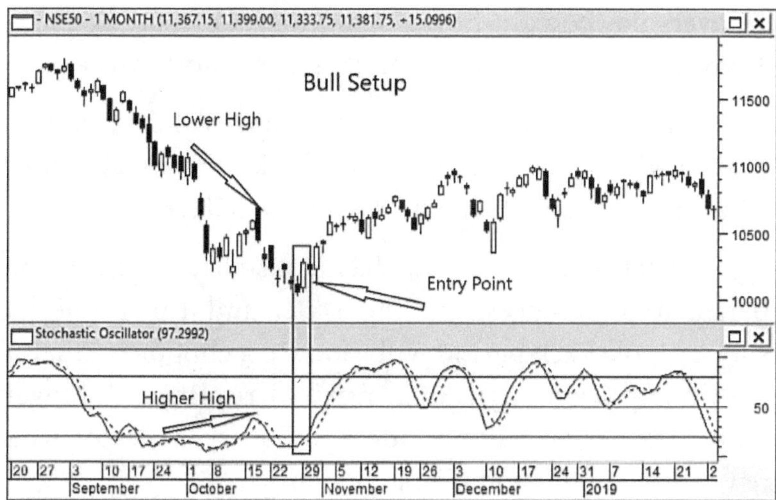

Similarly, in bear set-up, Stochastic Oscillator forms a lower low but stock forms a higher low. Even though the stock held above its prior low but Stochastic Oscillator shows increasing downside momentum. The next advance is expected to result in an important peak.

CONCLUSION

While momentum oscillators are best suited for trading ranges, they can also be used with securities that trend, provided the trend takes on a zigzag format. Pullbacks are part of uptrends that zigzag higher. Bounces are part of downtrends that zigzag lower. In this regard, the Stochastic Oscillator can be used to identify opportunities in harmony with the bigger trend.

The indicator can also be used to identify reversal near support or resistance. If a security trade near support with an oversold Stochastic Oscillator, look for a break above 20 to signal an upturn and successful support test.

Conversely, If a security trade near resistance with an overbought Stochastic Oscillator, look for a break below 80 to signal a downturn and resistance failure.

The settings on the Stochastic Oscillator depend on personal preferences, trading style, and timeframe. A shorter look-back period will produce a choppy oscillator with many overbought and oversold readings. A longer look-back period will provide a smoother oscillator with fewer overbought and oversold readings.

Like all technical indicators, it is important to use the Stochastic Oscillator in conjunction with other technical analysis tools. Volume, support/resistance, and breakouts can be used to confirm or refute the signals produced by the Stochastic Oscillator.

~~~
~~~

CHAPTER 27
Bollinger Bands

Developed by John Bollinger, Bollinger Bands are volatility bands placed above and below a moving average. Volatility is based on the standard deviation, which changes as volatility increases and decreases. The bands automatically widen when volatility increases and narrow when volatility decreases.

This dynamic nature of Bollinger Bands also means they can be used on different securities with the standard settings. (For signals, Bollinger Bands can be used to identify M-Tops and W-Bottoms or to determine the strength of the trend).

CALCULATION

Middle Band = 20 day SMA

Upper Band = 20 day SMA + (20 day Standard deviation x 2)

Lower Band = 20 day SMA - (20 day Standard deviation
x 2)

APPLICATION

Price move in trend, then consolidation happens and remain in range for some time and then again move. Bollinger Bands helps in identifying the consolidation period as at this point Both upper and lower bands come near to each other (The Squeeze).

This squeeze forecasts that a trend is about to begin. Bollinger band squeeze does not provide the direction of the move. but even the information that trend is about to begin or Volatility is about to burst is very useful for Option traders as Many strategies can be developed around it.

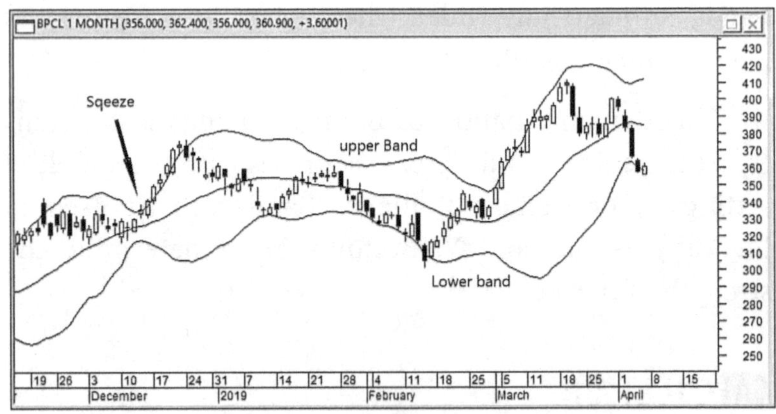


~~~
~~~

CHAPTER 28
Stop Loss

Let's face it. The market will always do what it wants to do, and move the way it wants to move.

Every day is a new challenge, and almost anything from global politics, major economic events, rumours can turn stock prices one way or another faster than you can snap your fingers.

It means that every one of us will eventually take a position on the wrong side of a market move.

Being in a losing position is part of trading, but we can control what we do when we're caught in that situation. You can either cut your loss quickly or you can let it loose in hopes of the market moving back in your favour. Even if once, it doesn't turn your way, could blow out your account and end your budding trading career in a flash.

The saying, **"Live to trade another day!"** should be the motto of every trader because the longer you can survive, the more you can learn, gain experience, and increase your chances of success.

Having a **predetermined point of exiting a losing trade** not only provides the benefit of cutting losses so that you may move on to new opportunities, but it also eliminates the anxiety caused by being in a losing trade without a plan. This is what we call "STOP LOSS"

Next question "Should you remain glued to Screen to execute the stop loss order?" No, it is not necessary as you can put it in the system as Stop loss order.

In simple terms, Stop Loss (or Stop Loss order) is an automatic order to buy or sell a stock once its price reaches a specified level, commonly known as 'the Stop Price'. The order is executed automatically, which saves you to constantly monitor your deals.

ADVANTAGES OF STOP LOSS ORDERS

Stop Loss orders are extremely important tools for traders. Global markets operate day and night, making it virtually impossible for a single trader to follow multiple deals on a variety of shares, commodities, currencies, and indices. Some instruments are extremely volatile and can experience huge price changes in a matter of hours, or even minutes. Stop Loss orders offer a simple solution to trader's need to carefully monitor changes and help protect a trader's balance.

Few benefits

- Offers protection from excessive losses

- Enables better control of your account

- Helps monitor multiple deals

- Executed automatically, at any time

- Easy to implement

- Allows you to decide what amount you are willing to risk

PUTTING STOP LOSS PUTS YOU IN A DISADVANTAGE?

Some trader feels that putting Stop loss means that the market will kick you out from the trade first, before resuming its journey towards your earlier set target.

Stop loss is a great invention for traders same as any other great invention such as electricity. If you use it properly, it is a blessing and if not, it is of no use.

Hence, The issue is not with Stop Loss but it's non-proper placement.

WHERE TO PUT THE STOP LOSS

Your stop loss point should be the **"invalidation point"** of your trading idea.

In simple words, you should place your stop loss order at a price, which if traded at, will change your opinion of the direction of the market. The idea behind this method of placing a stop loss order is that if the market reaches your stop loss Price, you will no longer want to be in your trade, so the stop loss will exit your trade for you.

TYPE OF STOP LOSS

1. Percentage Stop Loss
2. Chart Stop Loss
3. Volatility Stop Loss
4. Time Stop Loss

1. Percentage Stop Loss

Percentage based stop loss means that you decide your loss based on a fixed percentage of capital employed on a trade.

Suppose you fixed a 4% loss on any trade, let us observe following examples.

1.1 Traded Long

You have bought 100 nos. Reliance share at 1000/- thinking that it's price will go up, but in case of stock going down, you intend to lose only 4%. It means when Share price will reach 960/- (1000 – 4% of 1000 = 960), you will sell it, limiting your loss to 4%

1.2 Traded Short

You have sold 100 nos. Reliance share at 1000/- thinking that it's price will go down, but in case of stock going up, you intend to lose only 4%. It means when Share price will reach 1040/- (1000 + 4% of 1000 = 1040), you will buy it, limiting your loss to 4%. (Please note that you can sell your stock intraday only or you need to use Future)

Percentage based Stop losses are often triggered if they are too tight or expose you to higher risk if they are too loose.

How to properly use % based Stops, we will discuss it later under topic "Position sizing".

2. Chart Stop Loss

A more sensible way to determine stops would be to base it on **what the charts are saying**. Since we're trading on the basis of charts, we might as well base our stops on what the charts are showing us.

One of the points that we can observe in price action is that there are times when prices can't seem to push or break beyond certain levels. Often times, when these areas of support or resistance are retested, they could potentially hold the market from pushing through once again. Setting stops beyond these levels of support and resistance makes sense, because if market does trade beyond these areas, then it is reasonable to think that a break of that area will bring in more traders to play the break and further push your position against you.

Or, if these levels **DO** break, then there may be forces that you are unaware of suddenly pushing the market one way or another.

Chart based stops can be based on

- Resistance & Support
- Trend lines
- Moving Averages

Stop loss based on Resistance and Support

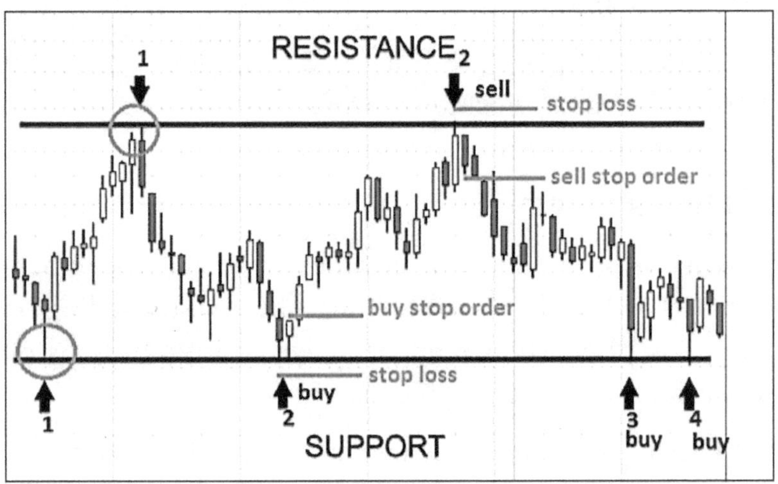

Stop loss based on Trend Lines

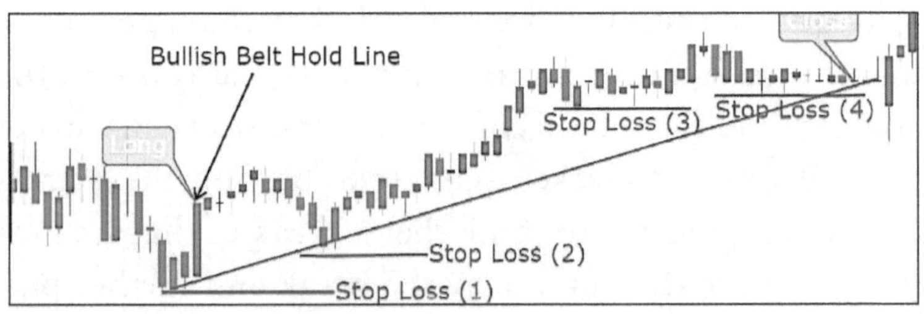

Stop loss based on Moving Averages

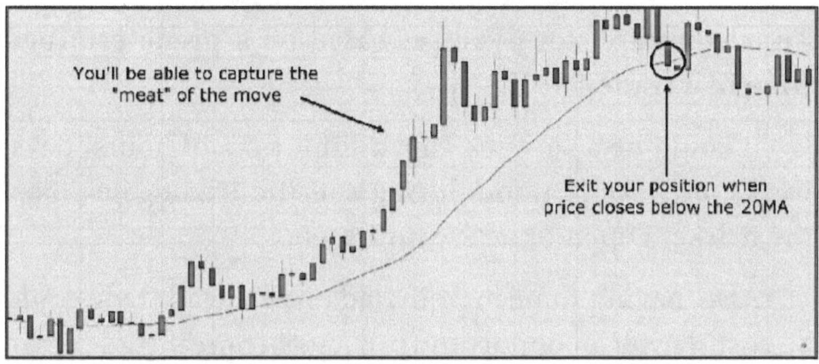

3. Volatility Stop Loss

It is a good idea to know the present volatility of the stocks and put your Stops further from it. You can use Bollinger bands or ATR indicator to get the information of the same.

Using Bollinger Bands

This can be particularly useful if you are doing some range trading. Simply set your stop beyond the bands.

If price hits this point, it means volatility is picking up and a breakout could be in play.

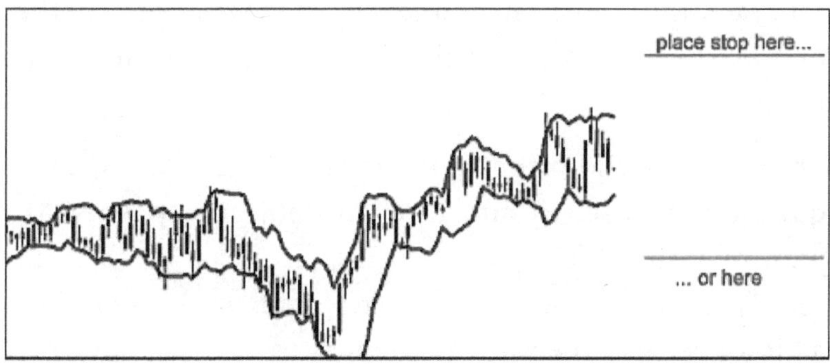

4. Time-Based Stop Loss

Time stops are stops you set based on a **predetermined time in a trade.**

It could be a set time (open limit time of hours, days, weeks, etc.), only trade during specific trading sessions, the market's open or active hours, etc.

Also, having some margin tied up in a dead trade could be costing you an opportunity in another great trade setup somewhere else.

Set a time limit and cut off that dead weight so that money can do what it is meant to do… Make more money!

RULES TO FOLLOW WHEN USING YOUR STOP LOSS

There are some rules which must be obeyed in all situations and adhering to these rules will make your life easier.

a. System Stop Loss Vs Mental Stop loss

Stop loss should always be in the system. Never put the stop loss in your mind as in the heat of battle, what often separates the long-term winners from the losers is whether or not they can objectively follow their predetermined plans.

Traders, especially the more inexperienced ones, often question themselves and lose that objectivity when the pain of losing kicks in and brings in negative thoughts like, "Maybe the market will turn right here. I should hold a bit longer and then it will go my way."

Manually closing trades leaves yourself open to making mistakes (especially during unforeseen events) such as entering the wrong price levels or position size, a power outage, a coffee break etc.

Don't leave your trade open to unnecessary risk so always have a Stop limit order in system to back you up!

b. Trail Your Stop loss

Once your stock starts moving in your favour, trail your stop towards its movement. It means if you are in a long trade, your Stop will move up and if you are in short trade, your Stop will move down.

Trailing your stop will reduce the risk and once it goes above your entry price, it will lock the profit.

Also remember the Golden rule that STOPS SHALL MOVE ONLY IN ONE DIRECTION It means following:

- if you have taken long position and once you have moved your Stop UP, in no circumstances, it will come down.

- if you have taken short position and once you have moved your Stop DOWN, in no circumstances, it will go up.

c. Don't widen your Stop

Once you decided a Stop point, do not widen it, Keep it at the same point which you have decided before entering the trade.

~~~
~~~

CHAPTER 29
Setting the Target

Setting a **target for stock trade** is the last important topic which you must learn to complete every stock trade setup. I am very surprised that many stock market traders do not prepare their trade in advance, using methods which include setting value that is expected to be reached during trade development.

This Target value is very important as it helps in two ways. The exact target of any stock trade helps to decide if the trade is worth picking and realization. The trade where risk is too big in comparison to possible reward is not a good trade and should not be realized. This predefined value allows using of the risk-reward ratio for this decision. (we will learn risk-reward in detail in the later topic)

The knowledge of this Target value is also a good stock market trading tool that helps to manage already opened trade. It helps to decide when is a good time to trail stop loss level and also when to take profit and close the trade. It is good to know when the trade should be closed.

A target for stock trade can be found by these two techniques:

1. Fixed price value

2. Moving (trailing) stop value

You must also estimate the time frame for your trade to reach the defined profit value.

1. Fixed price value targets

This way, you set a profit target for stock trade as fixed price values. These values can be set by these techniques:

(a) Chart patterns

(b) Retracements

1a. Chart Patterns

On the basis of Candlestick patterns, you can decide your target and stop loss. Observe the following charts, On each type, Entry point, Stop loss point and Target is provided.

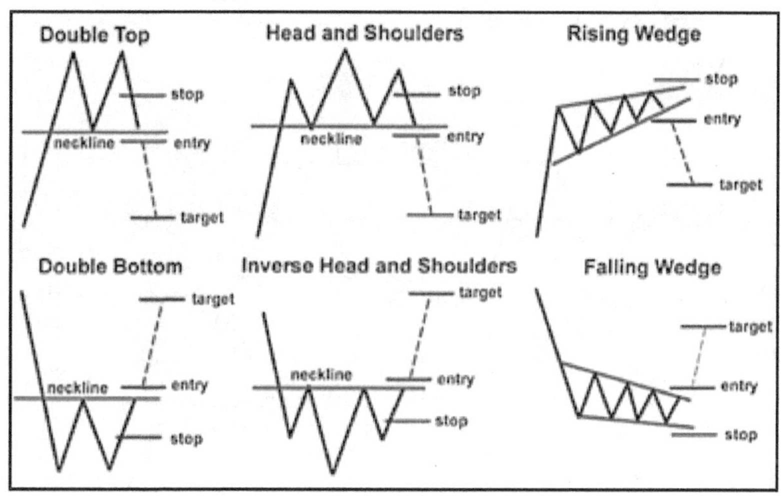
Double Top
stop
neckline
entry
target
Head and Shoulders
stop
neckline
entry
target
Rising Wedge
stop
entry
target
Double Bottom
target
neckline
entry
stop
Inverse Head and Shoulders
target
neckline
entry
stop
Falling Wedge
target
entry
stop

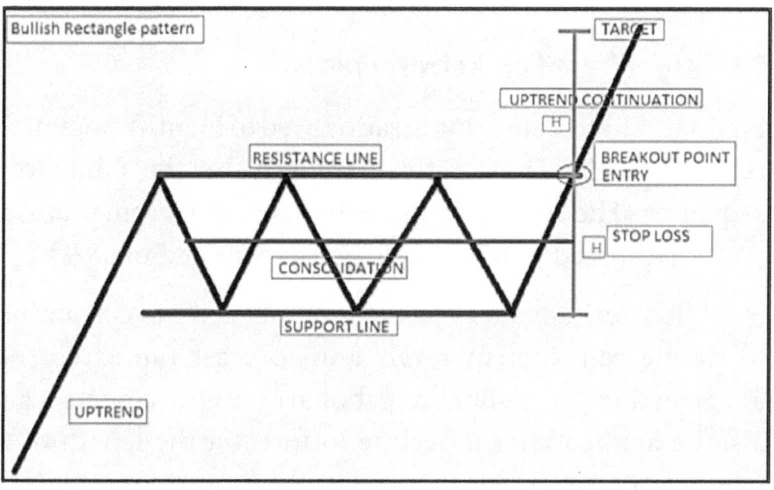
Bullish Rectangle pattern
TARGET
UPTREND CONTINUATION
H
RESISTANCE LINE
BREAKOUT POINT
ENTRY
STOP LOSS
H
CONSOLIDATION
SUPPORT LINE
UPTREND

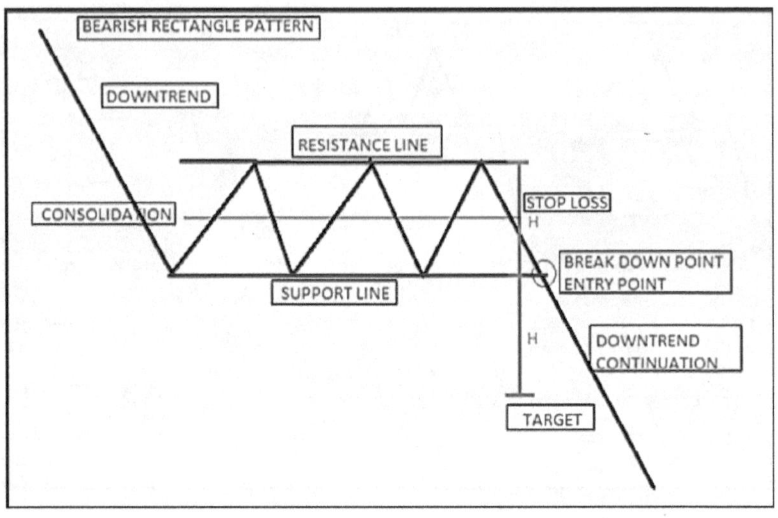

1b. Target based on Retracements

Fibonacci Retracements are ratios used to identify potential reversal levels. These ratios are found in the Fibonacci sequence. The most popular Fibonacci Retracements are 61.8% (rounded to 62%) and 38.2% (rounded to 38%).

After an advance, traders apply Fibonacci ratios to define retracement levels and forecast the extent of a correction or pullback. Fibonacci Retracements can also be applied after a decline to forecast the length of a counter-trend bounce.

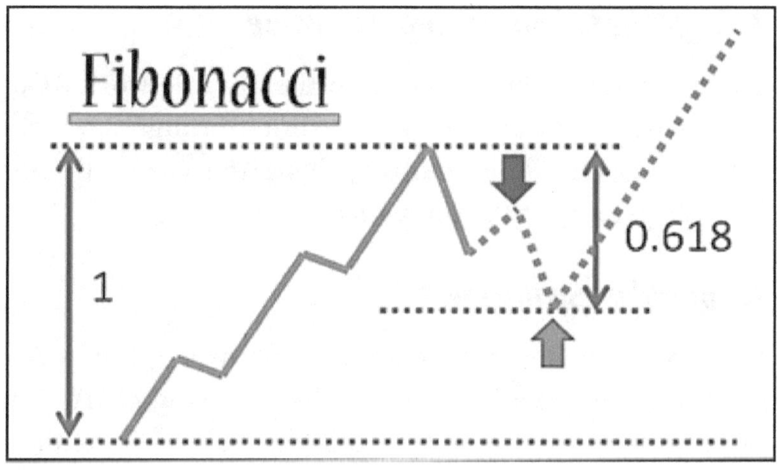

Here target will be 0.618 times of "1".

i.e if 1 is equal to 100 points, and you sell at upper horizontal line, your target will be 61.8 points.

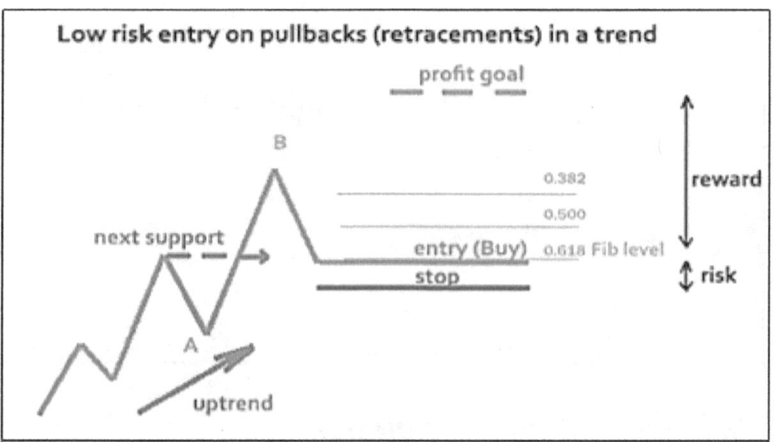

Here Target will be equal to AB.

2. Target based on trailing stop value

There is a very famous saying in the Trading world "Cut your losses soon and let your Profit running" You can achieve it by trailing your stop loss. You can trail your Stops as per any of the following:

2a. Based on Swing low

You can trail your Stops to retracement in an uptrend. You need to do it manually. look at the following chart. You can begin your trade with Stop loss 1, After few candles, when price retraces and started its move again, shift your Stop to Point 2, similarly shift your Stop to Stop loss 3 and ultimately, you will be out at Stop loss 4. By using trailing Stop loss, you can ride the full trend and earn a handsome profit.

2b. Based on technical Indicator

2b. (i) Based on Moving Average

Look at the following chart of Crude Oil which is a short trade. You can set your stop loss at 20EMA and trail it.

Once, the price closes above the 20EMA, you can come out from the trade.

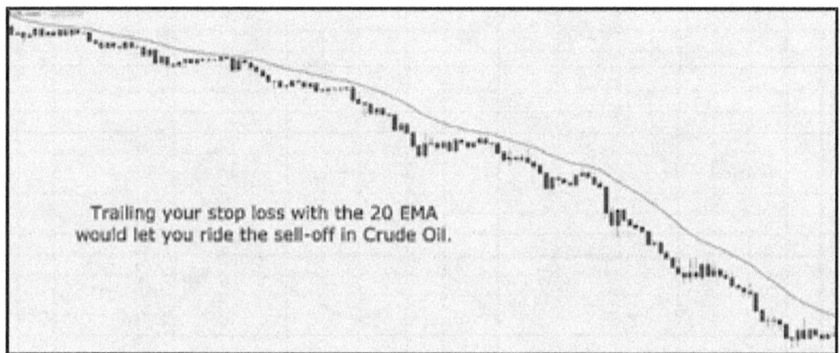

2b. (ii) Based on Parabolic SAR

There is a technical indicator called Parabolic SAR. It clearly shows the stop loss position. You can use this application and trail your Stop loss as per it.

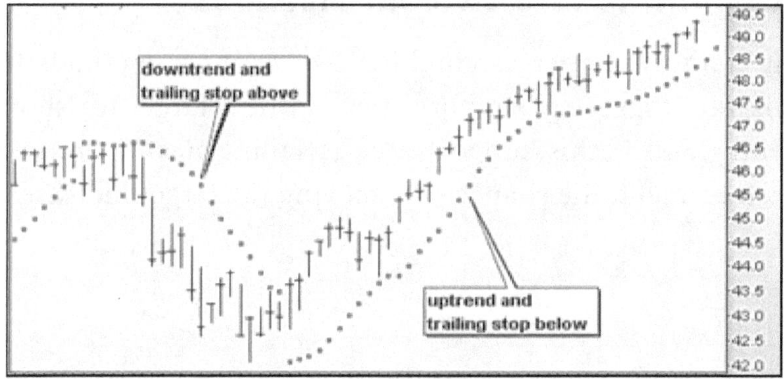

2b(iii) Golden Cross & Death Cross

If you are long in a trade, trail your stop loss as per death cross. Death cross means when 3 day SMA goes below 12 day SMA.

If you are short in a trade, trail your stop loss as per Golden cross. Golden cross means when 3 day SMA goes above 12 day SMA.

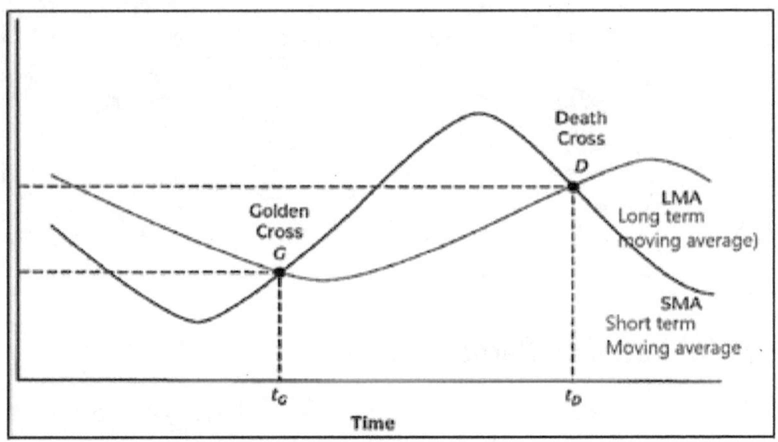

COMBINING TWO OR MORE METHODS

It is always better to combine two or more methods to fix the target. e.g. support area can be a target for short entry and if this support area is falling near Fibonacci retracement, the chance of achieving the target increases.

~~~
~~~

CHAPTER 30
Confluence of Indicators

Confluence stems from its underlying geographic definition which is regarded as the point where multiple flowing bodies of water join together to merge into one

WHAT IS CONFLUENCE

Confluence is the combination of multiple strategies and ideas into one complete strategy. Confluence occurs when two separate ideas/strategies are used together to form a Trading Strategy that is in line with the Trader's Risk Profile and goals. This term can also be used when doing technical analysis, by looking at charts and developing levels where different indicators are combined to help identify possible opportunities.

Technical analysts rely heavily on confluence to support their trading decisions. In technical analysis, it typically requires several indications of a buy and sell signal combined together to affirm a trade decision.

One of the most common points in technical charting where a confluence of indicators is used to determine a signal is at a potential reversal.

Reversals are commonly known to occur at resistance and support levels drawn on a technical chart. A price approaching a particular resistance or support line has the potential to reverse or continuing pushing through the trendline which can send mixed signals. Thus, traders will often watch for several indicators occurring simultaneously or within a short-term timeframe to confirm the trend through confluence.

Confluence in trading can be any, but not limited to following:

- It can be a trendline coming together at 61.8% or 50% Fibonacci level.

- It can be a support level meeting a rising trendline

- It can be a Fibonacci level meeting a support level where price meet

- It can be a resistance level meeting with Bear Engulfing candlestick pattern.

- It can be a Support level meeting with Bull Engulfing candlestick pattern.

- It can be golden cross occurring near Support Zone.

- It can be Death cross occurring near Resistance Zone.

Example of Confluence

Imagine this hypothetical technical situation in a stock:

- Occurrence of a bullish engulfing pattern – this suggests a long trade.

- A support level around the low of bullish engulfing – support indicates demand.

- The occurrence of a bullish engulfing pattern near the support area suggests there is indeed a strong demand for the stock and hence the trader can look at buying the stock.

- With a recognizable candlestick pattern and support near the stop loss, the trader gets a double confirmation to go long.

- Now along with support near the low, imagine high volumes on the 2nd day of the bullish engulfing pattern.

- The inference is quite clear – high volumes plus an increase in price confirms to us that smart Money is positioning themselves to buy the stock.

- With all three independent variables i.e candlesticks, S&R, and volumes suggest the same action i.e to go long.

In above, confluence is clearly visible, and trader can enter the trade with much confidence.

~~~
~~~

CHAPTER 31
Stocks Selection

As a swing trader, our focussed time horizon is as little as few hours to as long as few weeks. On this kind of time scale, fundamental analysis has little impact on a stock's price movement; therefore, stock selections are made using technical-analysis tools. Careful trade management is crucial to the success of this type of trading.

Although no hard-and-fast rule defines it, traders often trade in 20-30 shares and usually limit the number of simultaneous positions to ten or fewer. My suggestion is to initiate with only 4-5 stocks and give your time to understand their characteristics.

Stock selection is even more important for swing trading than it is for position trading. When you're looking for a stock to move right away, you base your decisions on selection criteria that are different from when you're positioning for a move that may last for several weeks to several months. Following are a few of the important selection criteria that swing traders use:

VOLUME AND LIQUIDITY

Swing traders typically focus on actively traded and relatively large stocks. The goal is finding stocks that are easy to buy, sell, and sell short. When trading time frames are short, you need to be able to execute your orders quickly.

Unfortunately, stocks with the greatest liquidity and trading volumes are closely followed by the largest number of professional traders, which usually constrains the number of profitable swing-trading opportunities, so swing traders often scout opportunities outside of the 25 or so stocks that have the highest trading volume and greatest liquidity.

TRENDING

Trending stocks provide the best opportunity for swing-trading profits. You may either use the *average directional index* (ADX) indicator. An ADX reading of more than 25 or so indicates a trending stock.

Volatility: Swing traders depend on larger, or more volatile, short-term moves for profits. As a result, they want to trade stocks that have histories of making large moves in short periods of time.

Sector selection: Just like position trading, swing traders try to trade long in stocks in the strongest sectors, and the weakest sectors are candidates for short sales.

Tight spreads: As a means of controlling slippage, you need to pay close attention to the difference between the bid and ask prices of the stocks you're considering as swing-trading prospects. Stocks with wide spreads make profitable swing trading difficult. Low-priced stocks rarely are good candidates for swing trading because the spread, as a percentage of the stock price, is usually too wide.

~~~
~~~

SECTION C

Money Management

CHAPTER 32
Money Management

You engage two amateur traders in front of the screen, provide them with your best high-probability back tested set-up. Ask them to take the trading position opposite to each other. You are sure that one who is opposite to your trading system will lose but to your surprise, both will wind up losing money. However, if you take two Professionals and have them trade in the opposite direction of each other, quite frequently both traders will be making money.

What's the difference? What is the most important factor separating the seasoned traders from the amateurs? The answer is Money Management.

Money management is like dieting and working out. Everybody knows it, but very few practice it in real life. The reason is simple: just like eating healthy and staying fit, money management can seem like a burdensome, unpleasant activity. It forces traders to constantly monitor their positions and to take necessary losses, and very few people like to do that.

Most traders begin their trading career, whether consciously or subconsciously, visualizing "That one trade" which will make them millions and allow them to retire young and live carefree for the rest of their lives. But the cold hard truth for most retail traders is that instead of experiencing the "Big Win", most traders fall victim to just one "Big Loss" that will knock them out of the game forever. Now, how to save yourself from this Big Loss and remain longer in the Market? The answer is correct POSITION SIZING.

~~~
~~~

CHAPTER 33
Understanding Position Sizing

Before we learn more about Position sizing, it is very important to clear "WHY" because once you understand why Position sizing is required, it will be easy to keep you interested in learning it.

OBJECTIVE OF POSITION SIZING

- To preserve capital
- To prevent any catastrophic loss from which one can never recover.
- To maximise profits with risking a pre-defined capital.

If we trade a size that is too big, we risk going broke. If we trade a size that is too small, we are limiting our potential profits. Thus, we want to find the sweet spot that maximises profits while ensuring the protection of the Capital.

What we want to achieve with position sizing is easy to understand. DOING IT IS THE DIFFICULT PART!

WHY POSITIONS SIZING?

Going from Rs 1 lakh to Rs 90,000 is easy in markets as it is just a 10% fall– but recovering from Rs 90,000 to Rs 1 lakh is not that easy – as that implies an 11.1% jump

Let us understand from following table:

Explanation of Row 1

Initial Capital = 1,00,000/-

Initial loss in % = 5%

Initial loss in Rs.= 5% of 1,00,000 = 5000/-

Balance Capital = 100000 – 5000 = 95,000

Target gain to achieve initial Capital Value = 5000

Target gain in % = (5000/95000)*100 = 5.3%

In following table, you can observe how much gain in % is required to get back to original Capital Value.

Loss/Recovery Figures in %		
Sr. No.	Percentage Loss in Position	Percentage Gain needed to Get back to Even
1	-5%	5.3%
2	-10%	11.1%
3	-20%	25.0%

Loss/Recovery Figures in %		
Sr. No.	*Percentage Loss in Position*	*Percentage Gain needed to Get back to Even*
4	-30%	42.9%
5	-40%	66.7%
6	-50%	100.0%
7	-60%	150.0%
8	-70%	233.0%
9	-80%	400.0%
10	-90%	900.0%

Let us go through the Row 6 and again understand through calculation that MORE THE LOSS, MORE THE PANIC.

Initial Capital = 1,00,000/-

Initial loss in % = 50%

Initial loss in Rs.=50% of 1,00,000 = 50,000/-

Balance Capital = 100000 – 50000 = 50,000

Target gain to achieve initial Capital Value = 50,000

Target gain in % = (50,000/50,000)*100 = 100%

Once, you lose 50% of your capital, you need 100% gain to reach the initial level and now you need to take the bigger risk for bigger gains. We call it "Revenge trade" and once you are into this type of trade, It will continue until you completely destroy your equity or somehow you just give up trading by blaming equities!

To constantly stay in the game, and to be able to recover requires patience, clarity and one more vital ingredient to our trading strategies – Position sizing!

In simple terms, position sizing is how much you should invest in each stock or strategy.

WHAT IS POSITION SIZING

Position sizing refers to the number of units invested in a particular security. A trader's total Capital and risk tolerance should be taken into account when determining appropriate position sizing.

RISK PER TRADE

Before understanding Position sizing, you must finalise Risk per trade, Ideally, you should not risk more than 2% of your total capital in one trade. e.g. suppose your total Capital is 10 lacs, then you must not take risk more than Rs.20,000/- (2% of 10 Lacs) Here, risk tolerance comes into the picture. If you are not comfortable to take Rs.20,000 risk per trade, you should reduce this amount to your comfort level. Let us assume it as Rs.10,000/- per trade (1% of your Capital). It simply means that even if you lose 10 consecutive trades, you will lose only 10% of your capital.

A thumb rule for knowing your risk tolerance is to observe your sleep. If you are not able to sleep peacefully with "X" amount, you must reduce this amount to "Y' level which allows you to nap comfortably.

Now to understand better, let us assume that we will take Rs.10,000/- risk per trade.

The success of Position sizing depends on the fact that you finalise your risk before entering a trade. It means, once you decide to enter a trade, you must know what is your stop loss. Understand it from the following examples:

POSITION SIZING EXAMPLE

1. Suppose, based on technical analysis, you get a buy signal of ITC at Rs.270/-. As, its long term support is at Rs.260/-, hence, you fixed your Stop loss at 257/-

   Now note the following carefully

   Entry Price = 270/-

   Stop loss = 257/-

   Risk per share = 270 – 257 = 13/-

   Risk per trade = Rs.10,000/-

   Total Quantity to be bought = 10000/13 = 769.2

   Total Quantity to be bought = 750 Nos. approximately

   Hence, as per Position sizing, you can buy 750 shares of ITC @ Rs.270/-

2. Suppose, based on technical analysis, you get a buy signal of ONGC at Rs.162/-. As, its long term support is at Rs.135/-, hence, you fixed your Stop loss at 131/-.

Now note the following carefully

Entry Price = 162/-

Stop loss = 131/-

Risk per share = 162 – 131 = 31/-

Risk per trade = Rs.10,000/-

Total Quantity to be bought = 10000/31 = 322.5

Total Quantity to be bought = 320 nos. approximately

Hence, as per Position sizing, you can buy 320 shares of ONGC @ Rs.162/-

POSITION SIZING AND GAP RISK

Traders should be aware that even if they use correct position sizing, they may lose more than their specified account risk limit if a stock gaps down below their stop-loss order. If increased volatility is expected, such as before company earnings announcements, traders should reduce their position size to reduce gap risk.

RISK TO REWARD RATIO

Risk to Reward Ratio is simply a ration between Risk and Reward. Here, Risk is the point difference between Entry Price and Stop loss and reward is the point difference between Target Price and Entry Price. i.e.

Risk = Entry Price – Stop Loss

Reward = Target Price – Entry Price

Suppose, based on technical analysis, you get a buy signal of ITC at Rs.270/-. As its long term support is at Rs.260/-, hence, you fixed your Stop loss at 257/- and its long time resistance is at 300/- hence you kept your target at Rs.300/-

Now

Entry Price = 270/-

Stop Loss   = 257/-

Target   = 300/-

Here Risk   = Entry Price – Stop Loss

Risk   = 270 – 257

Risk   = 13

Reward   = Target Price – Entry Price

Reward   = 300 – 270 = 30

Reward   = 30

Risk to Reward Ratio = 13:30

i.e. 1 to 2.3

Please note that here our Stop Loss & Target are not arbitrary chosen, instead, these are chosen based on Technical Analysis.

WIN RATE

Win rate is simply a ratio between your winning trade to Total trades taken.

Win rate = (No. of winning trade)*100 / (Total trades)

e.g. Out of total 10 trades, you won 4 (and lost 6). it means that your win rate is 4*100/10 = 40%.

You can achieve win rate of more than 50% if you apply technical analysis correctly. With more and more experience, you can increase it further up.

RELATION BETWEEN RISK TO REWARD RATIO AND WIN RATE

Risk	Reward	Breakeven Win Rate%
5.00	1.00	83%
3.00	1.00	75%
2.00	1.00	67%
1.00	1.00	50%
1.00	2.00	33%
1.00	3.00	25%
1.00	5.00	17%

Above table shows

- if you are risking Rs.3 for every Rs.1 gain, you need to have 75% win rate just to achieve break even.

- if you are risking Rs.1 for every Rs.1 gain, you need to have 50% win rate just to achieve break even.

- if you are risking Rs.1 for every Rs.2 gain, you need to have 33% win rate just to achieve break even.

- if you are risking Rs.1 for every Rs.3 gain, you need to have 25% win rate just to achieve break even.

Let us understand it further with the following examples.

Example 1: Risk to Reward is kept at 1:2.5

Assumption:

(a) You took 100 trades in 1 year.

(b) As per position sizing, you risked only 1% i.e. 10,000/- in each trade with total Capital of 10 Lacs

Case 1: Optimistic

(a) Risk to reward 1:2.5 i.e. you risked Rs.1 for a gain of Rs.2.5 in each trade.

(b) Win rate 65% i.e. You won in 65 trades (win rate of 65%). i.e. total loss trade is 35

Calculation of Profit

Total loss in 35 Trades = 35 x 10,000 = 350,000/-

Total Profit in 65 Trades = 65 x 25,000 =16,25,000/-

Net Gain = 12,75,000/-

% return on Capital = 12,75,000*100/10,00,000 = 127.5%

Case 2: Realistic scenario

(a) Risk to reward 1:2.5 i.e. you risked Rs.1 for a gain of Rs.2.5 in each trade.

(b) Win rate 52% i.e. You won in 52 trades (win rate of 65%). i.e. total loss trade is 48.

Calculation of Profit

Total loss in 48 Trades = 48 x 10,000 = 480,000/-

Total Profit in 52 Trades = 52 x 25,000 = 13,00,000/-

Net Gain = 8,20,000/-

% return on Capital = 820,000*100/10,00,000 = 82%

Case 3: Pessimistic Scenario

    (a) Risk to reward 1:2.5 i.e. you risked Rs.1 for a gain of Rs.2.5 in each trade.

    (b) Win rate 35% i.e. You won in 35 trades (win rate of 65%). i.e. total loss trade is 65.

Calculation of Profit

Total loss in 65 Trades = 65 x 10,000 = 650,000/-

Total Profit in 35 Trades = 35 x 25,000 = 8,75,000/-

Net Gain = 2,25,000/-

% return on Capital = 225,000*100/10,00,000 = 22.5%

Example 2: Risk to Reward is kept at 1:2

Assumption:

    (a) You took 100 trades in 1 year.

    (b) As per position sizing, you risked only 1% i.e. 10,000/- in each trade with total Capital of 10 Lacs

Case 1: Optimistic

    (a) Risk to reward 1:2 i.e. you risked Rs.1 for a gain of Rs. 2 in each trade.

   (b) Win rate 65% i.e. You won in 65 trades (win rate of 65%). i.e. total loss trade is 35

Calculation of Profit

Total loss in 35 Trades = 35 x 10,000 = 350,000/-

Total Profit in 65 Trades = 65 x 20,000 = 13,00,000/-

Net Gain = 9,50,000/-

% return on Capital = 9,50,000*100/10,00,000 = 95%

Case 2: Realistic scenario

   (a) Risk to reward 1:2 i.e. you risked Rs.1 for a gain of Rs.2 in each trade.

   (b) Win rate 52% i.e. You won in 52 trades (win rate of 65%). i.e. total loss trade is 48.

Calculation of Profit

Total loss in 48 Trades = 48 x 10,000 = 480,000/-

Total Profit in 52 Trades = 52 x 20,000 = 10,40,000/-

Net Gain = 5,60,000/-

% return on Capital = 560,000*100/10,00,000 = 56%

Case 3: Pessimistic Scenario

   (a) Risk to reward 1:2 i.e. you risked Rs.1 for a gain of Rs.2 in each trade.

   (b) Win rate 35% i.e. You won in 35 trades (win rate of 65%). i.e. total loss trade is 65.

Calculation of Profit

Total loss in 65 Trades = 65 x 10,000 = 650,000/-

Total Profit in 35 Trades = 35 × 20,000 = 7,00,000/-

Net Gain = 50,000/-

% return on Capital = 50,000*100/10,00,000 = 5%

CONCLUSION

From above examples, it is clear that if Risk to Reward ratio is maintained from 1:2 to 1:2.5; you will be a winner after 1 year even if you have only 35% win rate.

If you apply Technical Analysis in the real sense, your win rate will not be less than 50%. It will be around 55 to 60% and if you were able to maintain Risk to reward ratio more than 1:2, your Return on Capital will be in the range of 56% to 82%. Also, remember that we are not risking more than 1% of capital in a single trade.

~~~
~~~

CHAPTER 34
Keeping Records

The trading session has finished, now it is time for reflection and to review your trades. Depending on your trading frequency, it may be time consuming, but you must spare this amount of time to understand what went right and what went wrong during your trading journey so that you can increase your performance by analyzing this data.

THE TRADE LOG

All information regarding the execution of trades goes in the Trading Log. Later, when this data is processed into statistical figures and graphics, it will speak about the performance of the trader or system under the current market conditions. Logging your trades is time consuming and is less glorious part of trading, but if you don't keep track of them you will never be able to accurately determine if you have the ability to improve your trading performance. **The way your systems operate can be adjusted with these findings in order to achieve better results with your trade timing, position sizing or risk control.** It is especially tedious in the beginning when more discipline is required, but with time it becomes a Habit and effortless.

There are several items that are important to keep track of in a useful trading log:

- Stock name
- The time you entered the trade
- The price you entered the trade
- Initial Stop Loss price
- The Risk to Reward Ratio (R)
- The time you exited the trade
- The price you exited the trade
- The direction of the trade (long or short)
- Amount of points made
- Profit or loss amount
- Position size traded
- Comments: was there slippage, news announcements, a holiday, etc.

The above data will allow you to calculate other data like:

- Duration of the trades
- Which market session accounts for more trades
- Percentages of winning and losing trades
- Number of long trades vs. short trades

The Log provides critical data on where and how money is being lost or made. If trades are randomly made, for example, or deviate from one another in a significant way, it immediately becomes evident when looking at the equity curve or at the standard deviation of the results.

The most effective method for logging your trades is by means of a simple spreadsheet - by entering the data into the fields you create. It is worth keeping a complete and accurate log.

The benefits of a trade log do not end here: if your ultimate goal is to persuade investors and manage their Capital, this is a way to differentiate yourself from many others because this kind of information on statistical performance and reasons why and when you change your strategies are very important for the investor.

THE TRADING JOURNAL

Documenting your trading is of vital importance for tracking your trades not only in terms of "mechanical" data (Entry, Targets, Stops, Exits, etc.) but also in terms of the "internal" data as well, that is, the thoughts, emotions and other observations that accompany each move.

It is recommended that the journal comprises the specific information you need to accurately assess what you are doing well and what needs improvement. For professional traders, trading is a business and that is why the journal is part of the Trading (business) Plan.

This means that any detail of your trading decisions, including reasons for initiating, managing and closing a trade as well as notes concerning price action and market behaviour, should be part of your Trading Journal. **Although it is a time-intensive process, you will be astonished how the methodical way of maintaining a Trading Journal will give you a clearer focus.**

The more information you can pack into the journal, the better. But more importantly, be sure to put it in a way so that you can qualify the trades later on. Once you have a matrix in place of all of these different factors in your journal, you will see how quickly your weaknesses and strengths jump out at you.

Below is a sample list of points that you can easily duplicate for yourself. Feel free to add more points to it.

- Arguments why you entered the trade

- Arguments why you exited the trade

- Description of price action and market behaviour during the trade's lifespan

- The money management parameters: position sizing, risk control, management of the trade

- Did you do anything wrong on that particular journey?

- Any other thoughts that you had while trading should be noted, for instance:

    - Do I tend to make money at a particular time of the day or day of the week?

    - What price action Pattern are you trading best lately?

A bunch of conclusions can be reached by keeping a journal of your activity on a regular basis. For example, you may be surprised to find out your day trades work out 80% of the time while your positional trades only work 20% of the time. Or that every time you traded a particular stock, you lost money.

In this way, your improvement will be systematic and no longer the result of chance.

Wayne McDonell, a Successful Trader, narrates his experience of keeping a trading journal. It is really interesting how the journal became his judge and jury. Read below:

Was I a natural born trader? Hardly! I had the worst instincts and my gut feeling was always wrong. I think I was born the world's worst trader. However, my trade journal improved my trading right away.

I really needed this experience as well. I needed to get past my lousy feel for the market. I needed more control, and I achieved this by planning my trades. Then, by reviewing my trades, I learned from each of my wins and each of my losses.

The trade journal then became a check and balance. I found that if I wasn't certain about the trade setup, I didn't make the trade because I didn't want to have it put it into my trade journal. It was like looking over my own shoulder.

The judge and jury for my trades became my journal.

I would be too embarrassed to enter a bad trade into my trade journal when I thought it had the potential to be bad.

Because I entered all my trades into a journal, good or bad.

Source: "The FX Bootcamp Guide to Strategic and Tactical Forex Trading", by Wayne McDonell, p. 198-199

From the above quote, it seems like the journal is especially powerful when you tend to violate your system, as all traders are likely to do at some point. **A Trading Journal is much more than a routine of documenting and reviewing past trades. It is a strong psychological resource to give you more control over your performance.**

THE THOUGHT JOURNAL

A Thought Journal is that part of the Trading Journal designed to reveal destructive and constructive thought patterns. This same line of thought is found in Woody Johnson' articles:

humans are not naturally prone to accountability or self-discipline, which is why we need laws, rules, boundaries, and limits in society. Trading requires self-imposed limits and these limits must be created through personal accountability. You must know what you require in the way of protocols, strategies, and rules in order to create effective self-limits or self-control. Documenting actual behaviour provides the data to compare to your thinking and to identify strength and weakness - thinking precedes behaviour and behaviour reflects thinking. When you accurately record the thinking that was present during a trade, it exposes your actual state of mind, not the desired state or the one that we tell ourselves we have already. This confronts illusion about your true skill.

This is like a log of your emotions and behaviours. The best time to record your thoughts is during trading, or shortly thereafter, while the emotions are still fresh. As for what aspects to mention, it is less important than trying to record those which are meaningful enough to provide ways of improvement when reviewing them.

These are some sample questions to include in the Thought Journal. Take note that questioning yourself is the first step to awareness and change.

- Were there any environmental distraction during this trade?
- Were you tired during the trade?
- Were you overconfident in this trade?
- Have you noticed your unwillingness to cut your losses?
- Was this trade entered due to an impulse?
- Was this trade based on some tips?
- Was it a revenge trade?
- Is the need to make more money putting too much pressure on your performance?
- Are you having fun trading even when it is hard work?

KEEP A PRINTED RECORD

Many traders attach a Chart of their analysis and trade management to help them remember the trades when they review their trading journal.

Trading is in many aspects a very visual activity, specially, in its analytical and the strategic components. Therefore, keeping a printed record is one of the best educational resources a trader can develop.

This can be done simply by taking the screenshot of the chart and marking the strategic preparation of the trade and the key decision points. Relevant comments can be also be added.

The Best Of the secret is not only to record your mistakes but also to isolate objectively what you did best – what set-ups, routines, even extra trading activities which positively impact your performance. **The journal is not only a means of self-criticism; it is also a tool used to model your successful elements.** Record your best trades with printed charts and review them regularly. This way you train your subconscious to detect those particular price patterns which you traded so well.

The idea is not only to have a means of discovering the trader within you but also to make you excel. In fact, that is how you excel not only in trading but in anything in life.

Trading is relatively easy, but learning how to do it, well, that is hard work ... damn hard. Just ignore it if anyone tries to lead you to believe otherwise. But this hard work can be highly rewarding - and not only in terms of monetary gains. The satisfaction you get with the fulfilment of your Trading Plan is simply priceless.

~~~
~~~

CHAPTER 35
Trade Setup

We will develop few trade setup here. Please note it will give you an idea about how to develop the trade setup. Based on it, you can develop your own trade setup. As we are not using Future, hence we will be taking only a buy signal.

TRADE SET UP 1 (REFER FIG 35.1)

Assumed capital: Rs.10 Lacs

Risk per trade: 2% i.e. 20,000/-

Indicator used: MACD

Buy: when MACD signal for Buy occurred

Exit:

1. Our stop loss triggered.

2. Our Target of 2R is achieved or we get sell signal from MACD.

Stock: Tata Steel

Time Period considered: 2nd April 18 to 4th March 19

POINT 1

MACD signal date: 2.04.2018

Entry Price : 584 on 3.04.2018

Stop loss point: 568 (low point on 23rd March)

Position size calculation

Total risk = 584 – 568 = 16

No. of Shares bought = 20000/16 = 1250

Hence, we will buy 1250 shares

Total Investment = 1200 × 584 = 700,800/-

Risk to reward : 1:2

Hence target : 584 + 2 × 16 = 616

Our target hit on 19th April

Total profit = 32 × 1250 = 40,000/-

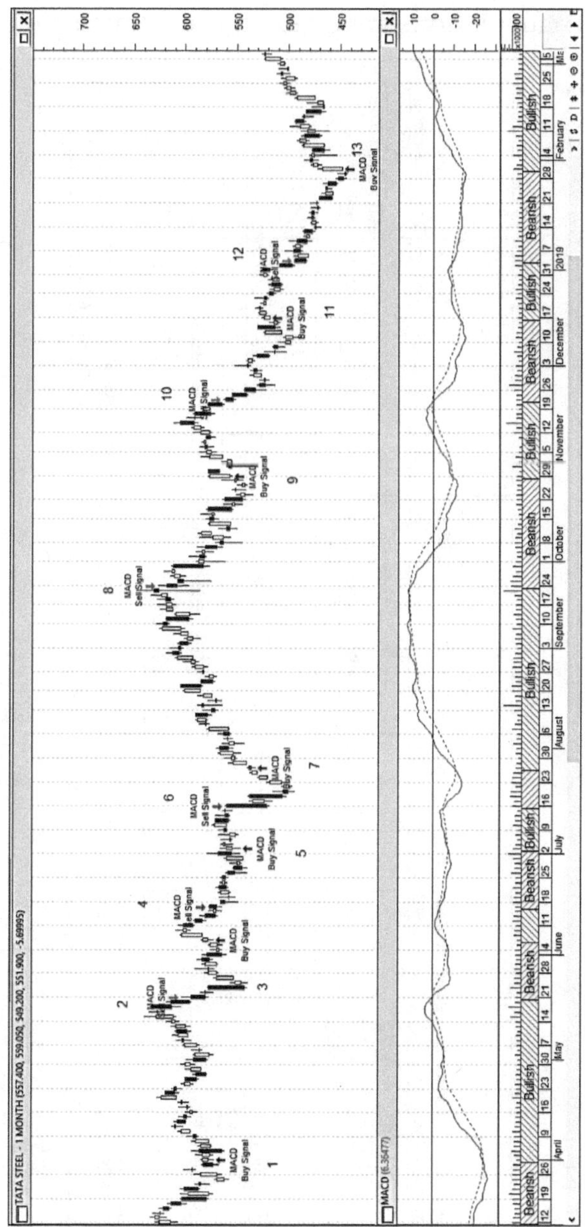

Fig 35.1

All calculations are given in the following table

Point Name	Entry date	Action	Entry Point	Stop loss	Risk	Position	Shares Bought	Target		Exit price	Exit date	Profit / loss	Remark
								2R	MACD sell signal				
1	02-04-2018	Buy	584	568	16	1250	1250	616		616	19-04-2019	40,000	Target 2R achieved
2		Sell	No trade										
3	06-06-2018	Buy	584	558.5	25.5	784.3137	780	635	563	563	18-06-2019	-16,380	Exited at MACD sell signal
4		Sell	No trade										
5	04-07-2018	Buy	565.6	539.2	26.4	757.5758	750	618.4		539.2	18-06-2019	-19,800	Stop loss hit
6		Sell	No trade										
7	26-07-2018	Buy	540	493.55	46.45	430.5705	430	632.9		632.9	19-09-2019	39,947	Target 2R achieved
8		Sell	No trade										
9	29-10-2018	Buy	No trade	Buy not triggrerd as stock did not cross MACD high next day									
10		Sell	No trade										
11	18-12-2019	Buy	526.05	507.5	18.55	1078.167	1050	563.15		507.5	19-09-2019	-19,478	Stop loss hit
12		Sell	No trade										
13	31-01-2019	Buy	472.5	447	25.5	784.3137	780	523.5		523.5	19-09-2019	39,780	2R achieved
											Net Gain	**64,070**	

TRADE SET UP 2 (REFER FIG 35.2)

Assumed capital: Rs.10 Lacs

Risk per trade : 2 % i.e. 20,000/-

Indicator used: ADX, Moving average, Stochastic Indicator

Buy:

Condition 1: When Stochastic give buy signal

Condition 2: When ADX slope is negative, it means though the price is going down & ADX is going down showing that the trend is losing strength.

Condition 3: When we get buy signal from candlestick pattern.

Exit:

When 3 days SMA crosses below 12 days SMA.

Or Our stop loss triggered.

Stock: HDFC Bank

Explanation

At Line CD, we can observe that ADX is reducing showing trend is losing strength and Stochastic is in the oversold zone. We await a signal from Stochastic and candlestick to buy

On the second candlestick, we get the buy signal both from Stochastic and Candlestick.

We decided to enter above line EF (2056.79) and support here is Line AB (1992.4)

Entry Price: 2057 on 21.06.2018

Stop loss Price: 1992

Risk = 2057 – 1992 = 65

Total Stocks to purchase = 20,000/65 = 307

Total Investment = 1992 x 307 = 6,11,544/-

Exit Point = 2190 (At Line GH, 3 days SMA crossed below 12 days SMA) on 25.07.2018

Total gain = 2190 – 1992 = 198

Total gain in Rs. = 198 × 307 = 60,786/-

% gain = 60,786*100/6,11,544 = 9.94% in 34 day

Yearly % gain = 9.94 × 34 / 365 = 92.5%

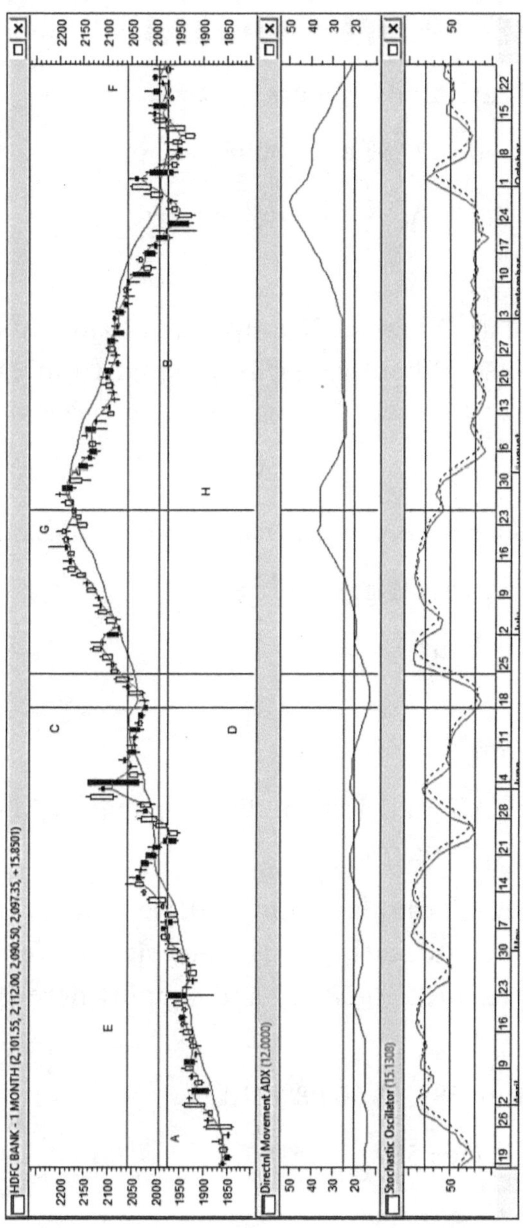

Fig 35.2

TRADE SET UP 3 (REFER FIG 35.3)

Assumed capital: Rs.10 Lacs

Risk per trade : 2 % i.e. 20,000/-

Indicator used: ADX, Moving average

Buy:

Condition 1: When ADX move from below to above 20. Condition 2: When we get buy signal from candlestick pattern.

Exit:

When 3 days SMA crosses below 12 days SMA.

Or Our stop loss triggered.

Stock: Axis Bank

Explanation

After Line AB, our first condition is met as ADX crosses above 20 from below.

After Black candle on Line AB, we waited till the third candle which is clearly giving a buy signal. We decided to enter above line EF (580.8) and support here is Line CD (539.2)

Entry Price : 589 on 06.08.2018

Stop loss Price : 539

Risk = 589 – 539 = 50

Total Stocks to purchase = 20,000/50 = 400

Total Investment = 400 x 589 = 2,35,600/-

Exit Point = 640 (At Line GH, 3 days SMA crossed below 12 days SMA) on 05.09.2018

Total gain = 640 – 589 = 51

Total gain in Rs. = 52 x 400 = 20,800/-

% gain = 20,800*100/235,600 = 8.8% in 30 day

Yearly % gain = 8.8 x 12 = 102.6%

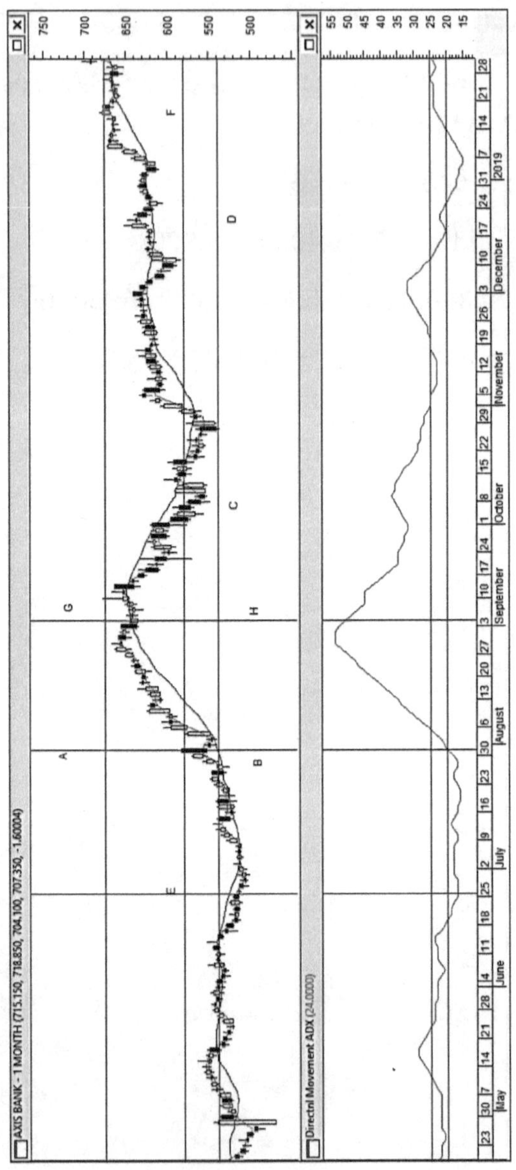

Fig 35.3

~~~
~~~

CHAPTER 36
Portfolio Targets

What are the reasonable profit targets for different stages? You may not believe the first target which I will give you for the first year. You want to make more money, and you should feel free to reach higher and do better if you can. These are simple yardstick which should help you see whether you're meeting the minimum requirements. They help you recognize when you are in trouble so that you can stop, think, and adjust your methods. If you trade for a Broking house and keep missing your profit targets, your firm will pull your trading privileges. As a private trader, you are in charge of your own discipline.

If this book helps you stop, think, regroup, and move higher, I will assume the purpose of this book is achieved.

FIRST YEAR

Beginner

The minimally acceptable performance level for a beginner is a loss of 10% of trading capital in first year.

Traders are generally shocked when I give them this number. They forget that most beginners blow themselves out in the first year itself. Many lose 10% in a month if not in a week. If you can survive for a year, learn about trading, and lose less than 10%, your education is cheap and you are way ahead of the crowd.

SECOND YEAR

The goal of a beginner is to cover trading expenses and generate an annual return on his account just more than long term Bank Return i.e. around 10%.

You have to add the cost of software, data, training classes, and books. Beginners often throw money at gurus who promise the Holy grail. Charging your trading related expenses against your account introduces a useful reality check. If you can cover them and then beat the Bank rate of interest for long terms, you are no longer a beginner!

THIRD YEAR & FOURTH YEAR

Now, you have qualified to Intermediate stage.

INTERMEDIATE (SERIOUS AMATEUR OR SEMIPROFESSIONAL)

The minimum acceptable performance level for a serious amateur is a return on equity twice the Bank rate of interest for long terms. Your improvement is evolutionary, not revolutionary. Cut some of your losses a little faster, grab some of your profits a little sooner, learn a few more tricks of the trade.

Once you are covering your trading expenses and making double what you could get from riskless bank deposits, you are miles ahead of the most of the traders.

The goal of a serious amateur or a semi-professional is to generate a 20% annual return on equity. At this stage, the size of your trading capital becomes an important factor. If you are trading with a Capital of 50 lacs, you may be able to start living off your profits. But what if you trade a relatively small account, say 10 Lacs, You know you can trade, but 20% of 10 Lacs is not enough for a living.

Undercapitalization is your worst enemy. Most undercapitalized traders destroy themselves by overtrading, trying to squeeze unrealistic returns from their tiny accounts. Take crazy risks, and you'll have crazy results—both on the way up and on the way down. Better stick to your trading system and leverage your skills by trading other people's money.

FIFTH & SUBSEQUENT YEARS

If you are able to earn consistently for 3rd and 4th year, you are now qualified to Expert level.

EXPERT

Minimal performance targets are more flexible for experts. Their returns are steadier but not necessarily higher than those of serious amateurs. You have to continue outperforming Bank rate of Interest. An expert may grab a 100% return in a good year, but by good planning, 40% a year is achievable and will be considered a very good performance.

The goal of an expert trader is to earn and put enough Profit into riskless investments to be able to maintain his current standard of living forever, even if he stops trading.

Trading at this stage becomes a game that you continue to play for your own enjoyment. Money does not matter so much and becomes a by-product of your trading. At this stage, you don't need to stretch for money. **Strangely, when you no longer have to stretch for the money, it starts flowing in faster than ever.**

GOING PROFESSIONAL

A beginner is better off starting with a relatively small account say around 5 lacs. Someone who has moved up to a solid semi-professional level needs to start pushing up his account size to increase profits.

Once you've moved up to the level of a serious amateur or a semi-professional trader, 25 Lacs will give you more freedom to diversify. Once you get your account up to 50 - 80 Lacs, you may start thinking of moving up to professional trading. These are absolute minimums, and if you can increase them, your life will be easier.

Starting with 5 Lacs, having 20 Lacs at a semi-professional level, and moving up to professional trading at minimum 50 lacs will improve your chances of success.

What if you do not have that much? Trading on a very small Capital raises the pressure to a deadly level. A person with a tiny account cannot apply the essential 2% Rule. If he has only Rs.20,000, his permitted risk is only Rs.400 per trade, which guarantees that he will be stopped out by market noise. A desperate beginner then puts on a trade without a stop and ultimately he ends up losing all his capital.

Trading with your own capital reduces the level of stress. Having to raise money increases tension and interferes with trading. Taking a loan is not a sensible way to raise funds because the interest raises an additional burden financially and emotionally. Borrowing money from family and friends has more emotional pressure as you need to justify their trust and trying to show off.

The capital which give you any pressure whether it is emotional or Financial or both, is bound to lose over time. If you have to worry about paying it back, you cannot concentrate on trading.

You are better off learning to trade with your own money. The time to use other people's money comes when you know what you are doing and want to leverage your skills.

There are huge numbers of Rich People around looking for competent money managers. Show a good track record going back several years, and you will have all the money you care to manage.

<p style="text-align:center">~~~</p>

SECTION D
Trader's Psychology

CHAPTER 37
Tune Your Mental Software

We have learnt about technical analysis & Money Management techniques in previous Sections. To become consistent winner, you need a trader's mindset. You need to understand the difference in psychological aspects of normal profession and trading.

I will take you through the process in developing the same.

FREEDOM AND DISCIPLINE OF A TRADER

Trading is basically without boundaries & market is a completely free environment. You are free to buy or sell, enter or exit, at any point in time. There are basically no rules that require you to either open or close a trade at any given price or time. Despite the fact that one of the primary attractions of trading is the complete freedom to make your own decisions and do whatever you want, whenever you want, the only way to consistently succeed in trading is to self-impose a set of rules to govern your trading and to practice strict discipline in following those rules.

What's the problem? The problem is that we all instinctively love having the freedom to do whatever we want and hate having any rules and restrictions placed on us, even those of our own creation.

Self-discipline is critical to winning trading. Unfortunately, self-discipline is typically the hardest discipline to come by. Most of us do a better job of abiding by the rules imposed on us from outside ourselves but we are not strong to abide the rules which we create for ourselves. Our attitude tends to be one more of, "Well, I made the rule, so I'm free to break it". While that's technically true, it's not an attitude that will serve you well in trading.

THE UPSIDE-DOWN MENTAL ATTITUDE OF A WINNING TRADER

One reason that losing is so common among traders is that many attitudes and principles that serve us well in life do not work well at all in the profession of trading. Unaware of this fact, most traders lack a basic understanding of what trading is all about.

In our ordinary, daily lives, we are taught to avoid risky situations. But trading is all about taking risks.

TRADING IS AN INHERENTLY RISK-FILLED ENDEAVOUR

Winning traders who genuinely accept the risk of trading have the ability to enter a trading opportunity without hesitation. They are also able to close a trade easily when it is not working. They are not burdened with the emotional pain that causes them to lose their focus or self-confidence as a result of a losing trade.

Traders who have not learned this attitude toward trading are driven by emotional reactions to winning or losing trades and have not truly accepted the fact that trading is a risk-filled business. Because they are not acting in harmony with reality, they do not make the best possible trading decisions.

Engaging in trading – and being successful at it – puts a huge demand on us, namely the demand that we maintain confidence while dealing with the continual uncertainty of trading in the markets.

In the profession of trading, facing the truth about what we're engaged in, is one of the key elements to success.

SUMMARY OF BEING A WINNING TRADER

Trading is a difficult game to master. Very few people become highly successful at it. However, it is possible for virtually anyone to become a master trader as long as he is willing to make the necessary effort.

Attaining the proper psychological mindset for winning trading requires rigorous self-examination and self-discipline. You have to learn to cultivate good trading habits because they aren't things that come naturally to most people. Making the necessary changes in yourself that will enable you to become a consistently profitable trader will more than likely affect how well you deal with life overall, not just how well you deal with trading.

Bottom line: Make the commitment to become a winning trader and that will enable you to become a winning trader. You can do it – but it's up to you, not the market, to put money in your pocket.

~~~
~~~

CHAPTER 38
Markets Most Fundamental Characteristic

Losing traders mistakenly believe that mastering the market itself is the key to winning. They fail to face the reality that the market can't be mastered. You can't control the market.

What you can control is yourself, what you do in relation to the market's actions. Winning traders realize this fact and put greater efforts into mastering themselves and their trading actions than they put into trying to master market analysis. It's not that market analysis isn't useful. It's just that the amount of available information available to consider, as well as the number of different technical or fundamental indicators, is virtually endless. Plus, what's significant at one point in time may be utterly insignificant at another point in time.

It's just all too much information to sort out and ultimately impossible to deal with perfectly. As a trader, your time is better spent on mastering yourself and your trading skills.

For becoming a successful trader, we need to understand Market fundamental characteristic so that we can align ourselves and grab the opportunities which Market throws at us.

MARKET CAN EXPRESS ITSELF IN AN ALMOST INFINITE COMBINATION OF WAYS

The market can do virtually anything at any time. This seems obvious enough, especially for anybody who has experienced a market that has displayed erratic and volatile price swings. The problem is that all of us have the tendency to take this characteristic for granted, in ways that cause us to make the most fundamental trading errors over and over again.

The fact is that if traders really believed that anything could happen at any time, there would be considerably fewer losers and more consistent winners.

How do we know that virtually **Anything can happen**? Let us go slowly here and establish this fact.

Let us dissect the market into its components and look at how each part operates.

- The most fundamental component of any market is its traders.

- Individual traders act as a force on prices, making them move by either bidding a price up or offering it lower.

Why do traders bid a price up or offer it lower? To answer this question, we have to identify the reasons why people trade? Here, you will agree that it ultimately comes to "PROFIT".

There are only two ways to create the profits: Either buy low and sell high or sell high and buy low. To be more specific, all price movement depends on 'what individual traders believe about what is high and what is low'. The underlying dynamics of market behaviour are quite simple. Only three primary forces exist in any market:

THREE PRIMARY FORCE IN MARKET

1. Traders who believe the price is low, will buy first and after some time will sell to gain profit.

2. Traders who believe the price is high, will sell first and after some time will buy to gain profit.

3. Traders who are watching and waiting to make up their minds about

Whether the price is low or high. Technically, the third group constitutes a potential force. You will be surprised to know that the reasons that support any given trader's belief that something is high or low are usually irrelevant, because most people who trade, act in an undisciplined, unorganized, haphazard, and random manner. So, their reasons would not necessarily help anyone gain a better understanding of what is going on. Now other method to understand is the fact that all price movement or lack of movement depends on the relative balance or imbalance between two primary forces

1. Traders who believe the price is going up (The Bulls)

and

2. Traders who believe the price is going down (The Bears)

If there's a balance between the two groups, prices will stagnate, because each side will absorb the force of the other side's actions. If there is an imbalance, prices will move in the direction of the greater force, or the traders who have stronger convictions in their beliefs about in what direction the price is going.

At any given moment, we can see who has the stronger conviction by observing where the market is now relative to where it was at some previous moment. If a recognizable pattern is present, that pattern may repeat itself, giving us an indication of where the market is headed. This is our edge, something we know.

But there's also much that we don't know and will never know unless either we are God or learn how to read minds.

For instance, do we know how many traders may be sitting on the side lines and about to enter the market? Do we know how many of them want to buy and how many want to sell, or how many shares they are willing to buy or sell? What about the traders whose participation is already reflected in the current price? At any given moment, how many of them are about to change their minds and exit their positions?

If they do, how long will they stay out of the market? And if and when they do come back into the market, in what direction will they cast their votes? These are the constant, never-ending, unknown, hidden variables that are always operating in every market.

The best traders don't try to hide from these unknown variables by pretending they don't exist, nor do they try to intellectualize or rationalize them away through market analysis. Quite the contrary, the best traders take these variables into account, factoring them into every component of their trading plans.

Because only the best traders adhere to the following three fundamental principles:

THREE FUNDAMENTAL PRINCIPLES

1. Consistently predefine their risks before entering a trade.

2. Cut their losses without reservation or hesitation when the market tells them the trade isn't working

3. Have an organized, systematic, money-management regimen for taking profits when the market goes in the direction of their trade.

Not predefining your risk, not cutting your losses, or not systematically taking profits are three of the most common—and usually the most costly—trading errors you can make.

Only the best traders have eliminated these errors from their trading. **At some point in their careers, they learned to believe without a shred of doubt that anything can happen, and to always prepare for what they don't know, for the unexpected.**

For a typical trader, just the opposite is true. He trades from the perspective that what he can't see, hear, or feel, must not exist. What other explanation could account for his behaviour? If he really believed in the existence of all the hidden variables that have the potential to act on prices in any given moment, then he would also have to believe that every trade has an uncertain outcome. Given the circumstances, not adhering to these three fundamental principles, is the equivalent of committing financial and emotional suicide.

Since most traders don't adhere to these principles, should we assume that their sole aim is to destroy themselves? But who does not love his Money? So, if financial suicide is not the predominant reason, then what could keep someone from doing something that would otherwise make absolute, perfect sense?

The answer is quite simple: The typical trader doesn't redefine his risk, cut his losses, or systematically take profits because **the typical trader doesn't believe it's necessary.**

The only reason why he would believe it isn't necessary is that he believes he already knows what's going to happen next, based on what he perceives is happening in any given "now moment." If he already knows, then there's really no reason to adhere to these principles.

Believing, assuming, or thinking that "he knows" will be the cause of virtually every trading error he has the potential to make.

Our beliefs about what is true and real are very powerful inner forces. They control every aspect of how we interact with the markets, from our perceptions, interpretations, decisions, actions, and expectations, to our feelings about the results.

It's extremely difficult to act in a way that contradicts what we believe to be true. In some cases, depending on the strength of the belief, it can be next to impossible to do anything that violates the integrity of a belief.

What the typical trader doesn't realize is that he needs an inner mechanism, in the form of some powerful beliefs, that virtually compels him to perceive the market from a perspective that is always expanding with greater and greater degrees of clarity, and also compels him always act appropriately, given the psychological conditions and the nature of price movement.

The most effective and functional trading belief that he can acquire is "anything can happen." If he believes that anything is possible, then there's nothing for his mind to avoid. Because *anything* includes everything, this belief will act as an expansive force on his perception of the market that will allow him to

perceive information that might otherwise have been invisible to him.

In essence, he will be making himself available (opening his mind) to perceive more of the possibilities that exist from the perspective of the market.

Most important, by establishing a belief that anything can happen, he will be training his mind to **Think in Probabilities**. This is by far the most essential as well as the most difficult principle for people to grasp and to effectively integrate into their mental systems.

We will learn it in greater detail in next chapter.

~~~
~~~

CHAPTER 39
Trading: Art of Perfection or A game of Probability

Eureka! Now, I found it. It's this trading room, or this service, or this indicator! Wait... something is wrong here. Not all of these trades are working and I have drawdowns! How can it be that this particular method failed and I actually had to take a loss? Must be something wrong. I will try harder and look for an even better system, a more expensive service, a new and improved guru, some absolutely no-fail software so that I can have only winning Trades.

Perfectionism can be a great help to people in many professions but can be fatal to a trader. Perfectionists, always trying to find the Holy Grail of trading, go from one service to another, from one system to another, looking for a way that they can be right all the time.

This is perfectionism in action.

Perfectionists are made, not born. We are taught from an early age by demanding (often in good sense) parents that we have to be the best in order to win their approval and the approval of others. Unfortunately, this is total upside down. Perfectionists share a belief that perfection is required in order to be accepted by others.

If you have a perfectionist mentality when trading, you are setting yourself up for failure, because it is a "fact" that you will experience losses along the way. If you cannot take a loss when it is small (because of the need to be perfect), then you will watch that small loss grow into a bigger loss and it will put You, the perfectionist into a vicious cycle of more and more pain. Your losses (that you hope will return to breakeven) will kill you.

Trading on hope does not work. **"The markets can remain irrational for a lot longer than you can remain solvent."**

The objective of trading should be excellence, not perfection. Moreover, it is essential to strive for excellence over a sustained period, as opposed to judging that each trade must be excellent. This is a marathon...not a sprint.

The greatest traders know how to cut the losses small and let winning positions run. Perfectionists often do exactly the opposite. They get in at the wrong time, stay in too long and then get out the wrong time. Perfectionists are always striving and never arriving. The market will find the flaw in a perfectionistic trader and exploit it day after day. The market is your greatest teacher and your most demanding critic, so take this wonderful opportunity every day to learn about yourself and make yourself strong.

If you see in yourself this trait of perfectionism rearing its ugly head, it's time to look yourself back, do whatever it takes to acknowledge it and then find a way to fix it.

You must begin to think of trading as a game of probability. However, very few can internalize and live by the true meaning of what it means to be a probability game.

Mark Douglas, the author of "Trading in the Zone", explains it well. Someone who masters the probability game produces uncertain outcome but consistent result. The best example to illustrate this concept is the casino business. The casino holds on the average 4.5% probability advantage to Casino owner over the player. It does not know whether the next hand will be a winner or a loser against the player, but the casino is certain that they always win given enough bets. Therefore, casinos do not care if a player is going through a winning streak, as long as he is not cheating.

Gamblers have to depend on luck to win because the game is designed with a negative edge for the players. When enough time and bets are played, there is no such thing as luck. Probability always wins.

That's exactly how you need to think about your trades. Market is random. Anything can happen to the current trade. A trader can increase his probability of winning either through fundamental or technical analysis but the best analysis can never produce a 100% certainty.

The crucial point here is – whether you have an edge or not. With the knowledge of technical Analysis & Money Management, you have a clear edge to become a consistent winner.

The key is that you must start with a trading plan with an edge of more than 40% win rate and RR of 1:2 or 1:3. You must back test it for a longer period to have confidence with yourself. As long as you continue to execute this plan over and over again, without worrying the outcome of each individual trade. The system will deliver the consistently positive results.

~~~
~~~

CHAPTER 40
Good Trade & Bad Trade

Please go through following and guess which is a Good Trade or Bad Trade.

1. You took a trade based on your trading plan and your Stop loss triggered giving you a loss of 2k.

2. Based on a tip, you took a impulsive trade and this trade resulted in a Profit of 10k.

3. You took a trade based on your analysis, you did not applied Stop loss. Stock went down below your stop loss, but recovered and gave you a profit of 20k.

Ans: Though, you lost money in 1, but it is a good trade. In spite of getting Profit in 2 & 3, these are bad trades.

If you think the opposite is true, you need to understand this chapter very clearly as this knowledge is crucial for you to become a consistent winner.

Winning traders know the difference between a "bad trade" and a trade that loses money. This is a critical difference to understand. Just because you end up losing money on a trade, that doesn't mean it was a bad trade – it just means that it was a losing trade.

What makes a trade a good trade is not whether it wins or loses – a trade is a good one as long as it offers greater potential of reward than risk, and the odds or probabilities of it being successful are in your favour, regardless of how it turns out. If you take a trade for good reasons and manage the trade well once you're in it, then it's a good trade, even if you end up getting stopped out for a loss.

Conversely, even if a trade happens to make money, if it wasn't initiated for good reasons and with a favourable risk/reward ratio, then it's a bad trade even though it may have happened to turn out profitably.

Winning traders operate on the premise that if they continue to make "good trades" as defined above, they will ultimately be profitable overall.

Losing traders incorrectly identify any trade that loses money as a "bad trade" and any trade that makes money as a "good trade," regardless of whether there was a reasonable basis for making the trade – and that leads to bad, losing trades in the long run.

Evaluating trades solely on the basis of whether they happen to be winner or loser, is doing nothing more than looking at random rewards similar to playing in a casino.

~~~
~~~

CHAPTER 41
Winning Attitude

Most traders when they first begin trading mistakenly believe that all they need to do is find a great trading Strategy. Once, it is found, they just need to apply it each day and the market will just immediately start pumping money into their account.

Unfortunately, as any of us who have ever traded have learned, it's not that easy. There are plenty of traders who use intelligent, well-designed trading strategies and systems, but still, regularly lose money rather than making money.

The few traders who consistently win the game of trading, are those who have developed the appropriate psychological mindset that enables them to be consistent winners. There are certain beliefs, attitudes, and psychological characteristics that are essential to conquering the world of trading.

TRADER'S ATTITUDE ABOUT THE MARKETS

Attitudes and beliefs about the market play a vital role in success of a trader. You must have a positive attitude about market. If you believe that the market is always against you. Such negative – and erroneous – beliefs can have a significant impact on your ability to trade successfully, therefore you can't hope to be able to objectively evaluate market opportunities.

The market is completely neutral – it doesn't care whether you make money or lose money.

TRADER'S ATTITUDE ABOUT HIMSELF

Our beliefs about ourselves are critical elements of trading psychology. **One personal characteristic that almost all winning traders share is that of self-confidence. Winning traders possess a firm, basic belief in their ability to BE a winning trader** – a belief that is not seriously shaken by a few, or even several losing trades.

Winning traders have a healthy respect for the fact that even their best market analysis may sometimes not match up with future price movements. Nonetheless, they possess overall confidence in their ability as traders – a confidence which enables them to easily initiate trades whenever a genuine opportunity arises.

In contrast, many losing traders have serious, nagging self-doubt. Unfortunately, if you see yourself as a losing trader, cursed with bad luck or whatever, that belief tends to become a self-fulfilling prophecy. Traders who doubt their ability often hesitate to push the button and initiate trades, and thereby often miss good trading opportunities. They also tend to cut profits short, overly fearful that the market will turn against them at any moment.

~~~
~~~

CHAPTER 42
Key Characteristics of a Winning Trader

Psychologically, the very best of traders share the same key characteristics, including the following:

TAKING RISK

They are comfortable with taking risk. Losing trades are simply part of the game of trading. Hence, It is very difficult to become a winning trader if you cannot accept losing trades. Winning traders are able to emotionally accept the uncertainty that is inherent in trading. Trading is not like investing where you keep your money in a savings account with a guaranteed return.

ADJUSTMENT

They are capable of quickly adjusting to changing market conditions. They don't fall in love with, and "marry", their analysis of a market – If price action indicates that they need to change their view on probable future price movements, they do so without hesitating.

DISCIPLINE

They are disciplined in their trading and can view the market objectively, regardless of how current market action is affecting their account balance.

CONTROLLING EMOTIONS

They don't give in to being excessively excited about winning trades or excessively despairing about losing trades Winning traders control their emotions rather than letting their emotions control them.

TRADE MANAGEMENT

They make the necessary effort and take the necessary steps to be self-disciplined traders who operate with strict money and risk management rules. Winning traders are not reckless gamblers. They carefully calculate potential risk against potential reward before entering any trade.

One of the most important psychological characteristics of winning traders is the ability to accept Risk and the fact that you may well be wrong more often than you are right in initiating trades. Winning traders understand that **trade management is actually a more important**

skill than market analysis. What determines profits and losses is often not so much a matter of how or when you enter a trade, but much more a matter of how you manage a trade once you're in it.

TRADE PERFORMANCE EVALUATION

Winning traders regularly review and evaluate their trading performance. They understand that trading is a skill that is only mastered through rigorous practice over time.

FLEXIBLE

Winning traders are flexible. They aren't ego-invested in their trades. They are able to always view the market objectively and easily cast aside trade ideas that aren't working.

CONTROLLING THE LOSS

Winning traders do not hesitate to risk money when they see a genuine profit opportunity based on their market analysis and trading strategy. However, they do not risk money recklessly. Always aware of the possibility of being wrong, they practice strict risk management by putting small limits on their losses.

UNDERSTAND MARKET'S UNPREDICTABILITY

Winning Traders understanding that the Market cannot be Predicted. Winning traders are aware of, *and accept,* the fact that the market is ultimately unpredictable, that there is no sure shot market analysis technique or strategy that will infallibly predict price movements. Because they are keenly aware of this fact, they carefully watch for signs that their analysis is mistaken, and if they see such signs, they quickly adjust their trading position.

In contrast, losing traders, once they have put a trade on, tend to only look for market action that confirms that they are right, and minimize or rationalize away any market action that seems to contradict their analysis. Thus, they often end up staying in losing trades too long and taking unnecessarily large losses.

~~~
~~~

CHAPTER 43
Life Cycle of a Successful Trader

I have found following article by an anonymous writer. How truly it describes the life cycle of a successful trader. Go through it. You can relate yourself and will identify at what stage you are now. You can also foresee how much more efforts and time you will need to become a successful trader.

STEP 1: UNCONSCIOUS INCOMPETENCE

This is the first step you take when starting to look into trading. You know that it is a good way of making money because you've heard so many things about it and heard of so many millionaires. Unfortunately, just like when you first desire to drive a car you think it will be easy - after all, how hard can it be? Price either moves up or down - what's the big secret to that then – let's get cracking!

Unfortunately, just as when you first take your place in front of a steering wheel you find very quickly that you haven't got the first damn clue about what you are trying to do. You take lots of trades and lots of risks. When you enter a trade, it turns against you, so you reverse and it turns again, and again, and again.

You may have initial success and that's even worse because it tells your brain that this really is simple and you start to risk more money. You try to turn around your losses by doubling up every time you trade. Sometimes you'll get away with it but more often than not you will come away scathed and bruised. You are totally unaware to your incompetence at trading.

STEP 2: CONSCIOUS INCOMPETENCE

Step two is where you realize that there is more work involved in trading and that you might actually have to work a few things out. You consciously realize that you are an incompetent trader - you don't have the skills or the insight to turn a regular profit. You now set about buying trading systems and e-books galore, read websites based everywhere from India to the Ukraine and begin your search for the holy grail. During this time you will be a system nomad - you will flick from method to method day by day and week by week never sticking with one long enough to actually see if it does work. Every time you come upon a new indicator, you'll be ecstatic that this is the one that will make all the difference.

You will test out automated systems, you'll play with moving averages, Fibonacci lines, support & resistance, pivots, fractals, divergences, DMI, ADX, and a hundred other things all in the vein

You hope that your 'magic system' starts today. You will also become a top and bottom picker, trying to find the exact point of reversal with your indicators and you'll find yourself chasing losing trades and even adding to them because you are so sure you are right.

You'll go into the live chat room and see other traders making profits and you want to know why it's not you - you'll ask a million questions, some of which are so dumb that looking back you feel a bit silly. You'll then reach the point where you think all the ones who say they are making profits are all liars - they can't be making that amount because you've studied and you don't make that, you know as much as they do and they must be lying. But they're in there day after day and their account just grows whilst yours falls.

You will be like a teenager - the traders that make money will freely give you advice but, you're stubborn and think that you know best - you take no notice and overtrade your account even though everyone says you are mad to but you know better. You'll consider following the calls that others make but even then it won't work so you try paying for signals from someone else - they don't work for you either.

You might even approach a guru or someone on a chat board who promises to make you into a trader (usually for a fee of course). Whether the guru is good or not you won't win because there is no replacement for screen time and you still think you know best.

This step can last ages and ages - in fact in reality talking with other traders as well as personal experience confirms that it can easily last well over a year and more, nearer to three years.

This is also the step when you are most likely to give up through sheer frustration. Around 60% of new traders quit in the first 3 months - they give up and this is good - think about it - if trading was easy, we would all be millionaires. Another 20% keep going for a year and then in desperation take risks guaranteed to blow their account which of course it does. What may surprise you is that of the remaining 20%, all of them will last around 3 years and they will think they are safe in the water but even at 3 years only a further 5-10% will continue and go on to actually make money consistently.

By the way - these are real figures, not just some I've picked out of my head - so when you get to 3 years in the game don't think it is plain sailing from there!

I've had many people argue with me about these timescales - funny enough none of them have been trading for more than 3 years - if you think you know better - then ask on a board for someone who's been trading 5 years and ask them how long it takes to become fully 100% proficient. Sure, I guess there will be exceptions to the rule - but I haven't met any yet.

Eventually you do begin to come out of this phase. You've probably committed more time and money than you ever thought you would, lost 2 or 3 loaded accounts and all but given up maybe 3 or 4 times but now it is in your blood.

One day – in a split-second moment, you will enter stage 3.

STEP 3: THE EUREKA MOMENT

Towards the end of stage two you begin to realize that it's not the system that is making the difference. You realize that it is actually possible to make money with a simple moving average and nothing else If you can get your head and money management right. You start to read books on the psychology of trading and identify with the characters portrayed in those books and finally comes the eureka moment.

This eureka moment causes a new connection to be made in your brain. You suddenly realize that neither you, nor anyone else can accurately predict what the market will do in the next ten seconds, never mind the next 20 minutes. Because of this revelation you stop taking any notice of what anyone thinks - what this news item will do, and what that event will do to the markets. You become an individual with your own method of trading. You start to work just one system that you mold to your own way of trading, you're starting to get happy and you define your risk threshold.

You start to take every trade that your 'edge' shows has a good probability of winning with. When the trade turns bad you don't get angry or even because you know in your head that as you couldn't possibly predict it it isn't your fault - as soon as you realize that the trade is bad you close it. The next trade or the one after it or the one after that will have higher odds of success because you know your system works. You stop looking at trading results from a trade-to-trade perspective and start to look at weekly figures knowing that one bad trade does not make a system poor.

You have realized in an instant that the trading game is about one thing - consistency of your 'edge' and your discipline to take all the trades no matter what, as you know the probabilities stack in your favour.

You learn about proper money management and leverage - risk of account etc. - and this time it actually soaks in and you think back to those who advised the same thing a year ago with a smile. You weren't ready then but you are now. The eureka moment came the moment you truly accepted that you cannot predict the market.

STEP 4: CONSCIOUS COMPETENCE

You are making trades whenever your system tells you to. You take losses just as easily as you take wins. You now let your winners run to their conclusion fully accepting the risk and knowing that your system makes more money than it loses and when you're on a loser you close it swiftly with little pain to your account.

You are now at a point where at a minimum you break even - day in day out. You will have weeks where you make big money and other weeks where you lose big money – but overall you are breaking even and not losing money anymore. You are now conscious of the fact that you are making calls that are generally good and you are getting respect from other traders as you chat the day away. You still have to work at it and think about your trades but as this continues, you begin to make more money than you lose consistently.

You'll start the day on a big win, take a big loss and have no feelings that you've given those profits back because you know that it will come back again. You will slowly begin to make consistent profits week in and week out.

STEP 5: UNCONSCIOUS COMPETENCE

Now we're cooking - just like driving a car, every day you get in your seat and trade. You do everything now on an unconscious level. You are running on autopilot. You start to pick the really big trades and getting big profits in a day doesn't make you any more excited that getting none. You see the newbies in the forum shouting 'go market go' as if they are urging on a horse to win in the grand national and you see yourself - but many years ago now. This is trading utopia - you have mastered your emotions and you are now a trader with a rapidly growing account.

You're a star in the trading chat room and people listen to what you say. You recognize yourself in their questions from about two years ago. You pass on your advice but you know most of it is futile because they're teenagers - some of them will get to, where you are - some will do it fast and others will be slower - literally dozens and dozens will never get past stage two, but a few will.

Trading is no longer exciting - in fact it's probably boring you to pieces - like everything in life when you get good at it or do it for your job - it gets boring - you're doing your job and that's it.

Finally, you grow out of the chat rooms and find a few choice people who you converse with about the markets without being influenced at all. All the time you are honing your methods to extract the maximum profit from the market without increasing risk. Your method of trading doesn't change - it just gets better - you now have what women call 'intuition.' You can now say with your head held high "I'm a trader" but to be honest you don't even bother telling anyone - it's a job like any other.

I hope you've enjoyed reading this journey into a traders mind and that hopefully you've identified with some points in here. Remember that only 5% will actually make it - but the reason for that isn't ability, its staying power and the ability to change your perceptions and paradigms as new information comes available. The losers are those who wanted to 'get rich quick' but approached the market and within 6 months put on a pair of blinkers so they couldn't see the obvious - a kind of "this is the way I see it and that's that" scenario - refusing to assimilate new information that changes that perception.

I'm happy to tell you that the reason I started trading was because of the 'get rich quick' mindset. Just that now I see it as 'get rich slow.' If you're thinking about giving up I have one piece of advice for you ....

Ask yourself the question "How many years would you go to college if you knew for a fact that there was a million dollars a year job at the end of it?"

Take care and good trading to you all.

~~~
~~~

Conclusion

You just observed that life cycle of a successful trader consists of various stages. These stages do not run parallelly, instead they run serially i.e. next stage shall begin after completion of the previous stage only.

You enter first stage unconsciously. As you are reading this book, it is evident that you are eagerly trying to improve yourself in this journey. Hence, you should now be in the second phase. In this stage, you must focus on deep understanding of candlesticks & indicators. You should practice trading taking small risk only. You must understand Money Management and practice it. Because successful application of Money Management only will take you to stage 3.

Once you enter in stage 3, you will realise that Trader Psychology plays important role in earning consistent Profit which I have explained in Section D of this book.

All of above stages are combination of following:

1. System/Strategy

2. Money Management

3. Trader's Psychology

Weightage of System/Strategy in a successful trading is 10% only, Money Management plays 30% and trader's psychology 60%.

You will find a lot of books on System/strategies as this is a really vast topic. Money Management is simple but it needs a lot of effort to apply the same.

You will find some good books on Trader's psychology, but ultimately it is on you how you behave in emotional situations. Consistently applying Money Management and proper Record keeping shall help you in improving your behaviour in those tense moments.

Remember only one thing "Any challenge which is not killing you (here I mean financially) will make you stronger. You are bound to get the success unless you don't quit.

I wish all of you to stay longer in trading and be successful.

~~~
~~~

Let's Evaluate

To know how much you have grasped the topics of this book, you must ask yourself following questions again.

Will I .....

1. Trade solely based on Tips

2. Define my risk before entering the Trade

3. Define my entry point and my Target before entering.

4. Take responsibility for the loss and do not blame the external factors

5. Execute the trade which I planned and will not execute any trade which was not planned.

6. Follow proper Money management in trading

7. Treat trading as a business.

8. Allot time to learn trading as any other profession e.g. Engineering, Medical etc.

9. Have a system with a set of rules which needs to be always followed.

10.   Be doing the back testing of the system to check whether it is offering any edge.

11.   Always keep the records of my trades

12.   Be making an effort consciously not to repeat the mistakes (a mistake means not following my rules)

13.   Be working on myself to improve/analyse

14.   Be reading enough books on trading (at least 1 in two months)

15.   Attend the Paid seminar on Trading

Circle all the responses that are true for you now. If you see your score improving from the survey which was taken at the beginning of the Book, my purpose of writing this book is obtained.

~~~
~~~

Basic Terminologies of Stock Market

Ask/Offer: The lowest price an owner is willing to sell the stocks.

Averaging Down/Averaging Up: When an investor buys more of a stock as the price goes down. Due to it, the Average cost of Stock decreases.

In the same way, When an investor sells more of a stock as the price goes up. Due to it, the Average cost of Stock increases.

Bear Market: A market in which stock prices are falling consistently.

Beta: It is a measurement of the relationship between the stock price of any particular stock and the movement of the Index.

Bid: It is the highest price a buyer is willing to pay for a stock. It is the opposite of ask/offer.

Blue Chip Stock: Stocks of large, well-established and financially-sound companies which hold a record of consistently increasing rate of paying the dividends over decades to its stockholders. Blue chip stocks typically have a market capitalization in thousands of crores.

Bonds: It is a promissory note issued by companies or government to its buyers. It speaks about the specified amount held for a specified time period by the buyer.

Broker/Brokerage Firm: A registered securities firm are called broker/brokerage firm. Broker's acts as an advisor for purchase and sale of listed stocks, they do not own the securities at any point of the time. But they charge a commission for their service.

Bull Market: A market in which the stock price is increasing consistently.

Business Day: Monday to Friday, excluding public holidays.

Close Price: The final price at which the stock is traded on a given particular trading day.

Commodities: Product used for commerce that is traded on a separate, authorized commodities platform. Commodities include agricultural products and natural resources.

Debentures: A type of debt instrument that is not secured by physical assets or collateral. Debentures are backed only by the general creditworthiness and reputation of the issuer. A debenture is an unsecured form of investment.

Derivatives: A security whose price is derived from one or more underlying assets. The most common underlying assets include stocks, bonds, commodities, currencies, interest rates, and market indexes.

Diversification: Reducing the investment risk by purchasing shares of different companies operating in different sectors.

Dividend: A portion of the company's earnings decided to pay to its shareholders in return to their investments. It is usually declared as a percentage of current share price or some specified INR value, usually decided by the board of directors of the company.

Day Trading: The practice of buying and selling within the same trading day, before the close of the markets on that day, is called day trading. Traders who participate in day trading are often called "active traders" or "day traders."

Equity: Common and preferred stocks, which represents shares in the ownership of a company.

Hedge: A strategy or an attempt in reducing the risk of adverse price movements of assets.

Income Stock: A security which has a solid record of dividend payments and offers the dividend higher than the common stocks.

Index: A statistical measurement of change in the economy or security market. Indices have their own calculation methodology and are usually measured as a percentage change in the base value over time.

Initial Public Offering (IPO): A company's first issue of shares to the general public. IPOs are issued by smaller, younger companies seeking funds for expansion and growth, but large companies also practice this to become publicly traded companies.

Internet Trading: Internet Trading is a platform with the Internet as a medium. Internet trading execution takes place through order routing system, which will rout traders order to exchange trading system. Thus traders sitting in any part of the world can be able to trade using their broker's Internet Trading System. The Securities and Exchange Board of India (SEBI) approved Internet Trading in January 2000.

Limit Order: An order to buy or sell a share at a specified price. The order will be executed only at the specified limit price or even better. A limit order sets a minimum price the seller is willing to accept and maximum price the buyer is willing to pay for it.

Listed Stocks: The shares of an issuer that are traded on the stock exchange. The issuer has to pay fees to be listed in the stock exchange and abide by the regulations of the stock exchange to maintain listing privilege.

Market Capitalization: The total value in INR of all of a company's outstanding shares. It is calculated by multiplying all the outstanding shares with the current market price of one share. It determines the company's size in terms of its wealth.

Mutual Fund: A pool of money managed by experts by investing in stocks, bonds and other securities with the objective of improving their savings. These experts will create a diversified portfolio from these funds.

Noise: In a broad analytical context, noise refers to information or activity that confuses or misrepresents geniune underlying trends.

One-sided Market: A market that has only potential sellers or only potential buyers but not both.

Portfolio: Holding of any individual or institution. A portfolio may include various type of securities of different companies operating in different sectors.

Pre-opening Session: The pre-open session is for a duration of 15 minutes i.e. from 9:00 AM to 9:15 AM. In pre-open session order entry, modification and cancelation take place.

Price Earnings (P/E) Ratio: A valuation of companies last traded share price to its latest reported 12 months earnings per share. For example, if the last traded share price of any company is INR 40 and earnings over a last 12 months per share is INR 2, then the P/E ratio of that company is INR 20 (=40/2)

Rally: A rapid increase in the general price level of the market or of the price of a stock is known as a rally. Depending on the overall environment, it might be called a bull rally or a bear rally. In a bear market, upward trends of as little as 10 percent can qualify as a rally.

Securities: A transferable certificate of ownership of investment in products such as stocks, bonds, future contracts and options which an individual holds.

Sector: A group of stocks that are in the same industry belongs to the same sector. An example would be the technology sector, which includes companies like HCL and Infosys. Some traders prefer to trade in a specific sector, such as energy, because they know the industry well and can better predict stock price fluctuations.

Smart Money: Smart money is the capital that is being controlled by institutional Investors such as market makers, Banks, funds, and other financial professionals. The populace perceives that the smart money is invested by those with a fuller understanding of the market or with information that a regular investor cannot access. As such, the smart money is considered to have a much better chance of success when the trading patterns of institutional investors diverge from retail investors.

Stock Split: An attempt to increase the number of outstanding shares of a company by splitting the existing shares. It is usually done to increase the availability of shares in the market. The usual split ratio is 2:1 or 3:1, i.e. one share is split into two or three.

Short Selling: It's a way to take advantage of a stock that you believe will decrease in price. After you sell short, you can buy back the shares at a lower price point and take the difference in price as your profit.

Stock Symbol: A stock symbol is a one- to four-character alphabetic root symbol that represents a publicly traded company on a stock exchange. Rural Electrification stock symbol is REC. while Infosys is INFY.

Trading session: The period of time from 9:15 AM to 3:30 PM is open for trading for both sellers and buyers, within this time frame all the orders of the day must be placed. Here all the orders placed in pre-opening sessions are matched and executed.

Volume: The number of shares of the stock traded during a particular time period, normally measured in average daily trading volume. Volume can also mean the number of shares you purchase of a given stock. For instance, buying 2,000 shares of a company is a higher-volume purchase than buying 20 shares.

Volatility: The price movements of a stock or the stock market as a whole. Highly volatile stocks are those with extreme daily up and down movements and wide intraday trading ranges. This is often common with stocks that are thinly traded or have low trading volumes.

Yield: It is the measure of return on investments in terms of percentage. Stock yield is calculated by dividing the current price of the share by the annual dividend paid by the company for that share. For example, if the current price of the share is INR 100 and the dividend paid is INR 5 per share annually, then the stock yield is 5%.

~~~
~~~

Bibliography

Trading in the Zone by Mark Douglas

Come into my trading room by Elder Alexander

Super Trader by Van K Tharp

http://learningcenter.fxstreet.com

www.thebalance.com

www.investopedia.com

corporatefinanceinstitute.com

stockscharts.com

www.tradeciety.com/common-trading-mistakes/

zerodha.com


~~~
~~~

*If you wish to get trained personally
from Author, please visit the website
www.tradingskool.com for details about
training dates in coming days.*